Catherine Kidw

"I Couldn't
Put it Down"

How to Write Quality Fiction
in Ten Easy Lessons

Media Productions and Marketing

ISBN 0-939644-20-7

Library of Congress #86-60701

Copyright © 1986 Catherine Kidwell

Cover design by Tony Schappaugh
Book design by Tony Schappaugh

Manufactured in USA

First Edition, First Printing

Media Publishing and Marketing, Inc.
2440 "O" Street #202
Lincoln, Nebraska 68510

How To Use This Book

"*I Couldn't Put It Down*" is meant to be used as an informative and entertaining guideline to the structuring of a piece of fiction. It is a "how to" based on "**how** I did," and is designed to function in either of two types of study.

As a classroom tool, it can serve as a practical written manual, with week to week progression and assignments to be used along with outside of class writing, the results shared and discussed in class. It has been deliberately made brief and concise because students in a writing class should spend most of their study time writing, not reading.

I am equally interested in speaking to all the adults who have always wanted to write a book, but don't know how to get started. Each point of technique is clarified by the use of specific examples so it can be understood by persons working without a teacher. The assignments can be completed, and the stories developed through unsupervised home study.

This volume is dedicated
to the constant man in my life—
my first-born, Chris.

Contents

Introduction

Millions of ordinary looking people are walking around guarding the secret that a great piece of fiction lurks in their brains. Like Michelangelo's statues, it will be released someday when they find the time to let it out. They each know something that nobody else knows—stories that nobody else could tell the way they could tell them. The greatest stories come from somebody's need to communicate how it was, how it felt, how it changed someone. The surprise will be that if they find the secret of communication, they will discover a world of others who will be thrilled to read and say, "I know what you mean, I have felt such emotion, dreamed such dreams, even though I am far away, and my life is different."

The stories in your head will never be literature until you write them down. Fiction writing is, of course, creative lying where the real facts are changed, embroidered, extended to make a good story. Even pure fantasy can be made to speak to real human emotions.

Writing is an art, and there are no unbreakable rules for creating art. However, there are certain basic guidelines of structure. Understanding them can save you hours of searching on your own. They can make the difference between amateur and professional work, between trite and quality writing.

Technique is a tool, very useful to the writer who can provide the other two basic requirements to success: talent and hard work. You must be born with some talent, but hard work and technical skill could be more relevant than the quantity of talent with which you were born—unless you have no talent at all, or you are a genius.

You may write well instinctively. If you have read a lot (and most writers have), you have developed an ear for how things should sound; but a basic understanding of technique can provide answers when you know it doesn't sound right, but don't know why.

There is no shortcut around the hours that must be spent getting it down. Writers have to write—and rewrite. There can be great joy in polishing your creation until it shines.

I wrote the popular novel, *The Woman I Am*, which later evolved into *Dear Stranger*, while I was a student at the University of Nebraska-Lincoln. I had enrolled as a freshman at a time when both my children were students at the university also. These novels reflect years of living, but I had never been able to pass along my stories until I had some practical guidance in how to build a piece of fiction, how to communicate feelings as well as plot to my readers. *Dear Stranger* is a story I made up, placing my protagonist, Bonnie, in settings and situations similar to ones I had experienced. I had always wanted to be an "author" when I grew up, but I didn't know how to get started after I became old enough to realize my writing didn't sound like Mary Roberts Rinehart's.

I have been teaching adult students how to write fiction at Lincoln Southeast Community College since 1976. I wrote my own text to show them in the simplest way some of the most important, practical guidelines that I had finally learned from a good teacher, and from my own six years' experience in creating *Dear Stranger*. *I Couldn't Put It Down* is a compact, simple statement of basic fiction writing technique. Most of my students are, as I was for many years, adults with talent and ideas, not sure how to structure them into a real story. These writers may have heard about conflict and point of view, but can they define the terms, or put them to use? When does a piece of fiction become a story? How do writers touch readers, and draw them into the action?

I would like to suggest to the person working without a teacher that you look about you for others who are writing or want to write on their own. You can form your own Writers Group (two people can start one). Sharing your work with interested comrades is a form of publication. It will give you feedback that has many benefits. You may not (and should not) always act on their suggestions or criticism, but reaction from readers can be very helpful.

This is a short book, not intended for speed reading. Read it carefully and refer back often as every line is important. If I don't preface every statement with a qualifier (usually, probably) you will understand that these terms may apply. Rules can be broken and revised if the writer is making an informed choice.

In this volume I will be using many examples from *Dear Stranger*. I will clarify the principles I am discussing by showing how I applied them in writing my own best seller. Using my own work as an example frees me to explain without question the author's intentions, and to rewrite where I please to provide bad examples.

Reread all examples until you understand them. Complete all assignments, not just approximately in your head, but fully written out. Only by putting guidelines into practice will you learn them.

Your reading all of *Dear Stranger* in advance would make this volume more interesting, but if you cannot do this you will still be able to understand the examples through the excerpts that are furnished herewith. *Dear Stranger* is a story of human relationships. The opening chapters are concerned with young romance, which may not be your genre, but the same rules for good writing apply to all types of well-executed fiction.

Fiction writing technique is not an extensive subject, despite all the long, wordy volumes that have been written about it. I would be pleased to think that this explanation of some of the mechanics, complete with examples and practice assignments, will help to open the gates of self-expression for many writers beyond my classes at Lincoln Southeast Community College.

Dear Stranger made best seller lists, has been published in foreign countries, and has prompted readers over and again to say to me, "I couldn't put it down." I am about to show you how to tell *your* story so that readers can't put it down.

What to
Write About

Character, Theme, Plot

Most good fiction has autobiographical roots of some kind. This does not mean that it is a true story. It may begin with a real event that is followed by the thought, "What if it had happened this way instead?" It may take place in a time and setting that you remember (as was the case for me in Part I of *Dear Stranger*). It may be characters experiencing some basic emotions you have experienced, but in a different story frame. Some truth allows you to more fully identify with a point of view character, and will produce a more realistic piece of fiction than one coming entirely from the imagination. Of course, you must also allow your imagination a wide range. Don't be restricted by the truth, afraid to try something new.

You are going to write a story. In order to be a story, and not a sketch, it must contain three definable elements: character, theme and plot. One of these elements spawned your story idea; and one (not necessarily the same element) will be more important than the other two in the finished product.

The Woman I Am began with a plot idea.

Plot and Conflict

A couple met in the unique, isolated World War II years in a midwestern air base town to have a brief but intense love affair. They lost all contact by the end of the war. Thirty years later they came together accidentally in a private moment, both married to someone else and far away from the complications of their now humdrum lives.

Conflicts: Part I (1940s):
War versus young love
Clock running out of time to be together

Part II (1970s):
Rekindled old love versus family ties and responsibilities
Clock running out of time left to live

Character and Setting

I chose to make the woman the protagonist, so the war was presented from the home front, not the battlefield.

Theme

Love *can* last through the years.

The Woman I Am was edited and published in accord with this theme as a paperback original by Dell Publishing Co., New York, 1979.

In my own mind, however, as the novel grew, the life of the limited point of view character, Bonnie, became more important than the love story and I came to see the structure growing out of the element of character.

Character

A woman, middle aged in the 1970s, young in the unique World War II years. A product of the social values of her era—a nice girl, becoming a homemaker, corporate wife, protester's mother.

The long time span made this an historical novel. Wars, elections, songs and (because of the focus on the woman character) sociological mores and changes for women, made a useful framework for nostalgia and reader identification. The character grew and changed, not only because she was older, but because she was awakened to the way the world was changing.

Conflicts

Internal: Conformity vs. self-development. Making choices from ingrained ideas about virtue, sacrifice, the expected role of woman.

External: 1. Two wars causing lack of control, uncertainty about the future.

2. Social pressure to conform to society's prototypes.

New Theme

It is never too late. A woman can continue to grow until she assumes control of her own life.

I could have begun with each of the two themes mentioned above and come up with two very different books. As it was, the combination of romantic and feminist themes gave an unusual thrust.

Despite discouragement from my Dell romance editor, I wrote a sequel strengthening the second theme. The sequel showed what happened to Bonnie after her reunion with John in 1975. I expanded *The Woman I Am*; combined the two books; and published the complete, longer novel as *Dear Stranger*, in hard cover with Warner Books, New York, 1983. The paperback edition of *Dear Stranger* was published by Warner Books in 1984.

Assignment:

Read the following opening pages of *Dear Stranger* from Part I,
THE FORTIES.

Excerpt from *Dear Stranger*

One

She was young in 1943—when the girls were red-lipped and virginal, and the measure of time was the duration.

That Friday, the February wind hurtled around buildings and scooted across the dirty snow that had packed down and refrozen after dark. Bonnie and her best friend scurried into the protection of the heavy revolving door and pushed it, groaning and resisting, to deliver themselves into the warm confusion of the Wheatland Hotel's Comanche Room.

The wind had polished their skin pink and fringed their high hairdos, but the little felt hats perched on the crowns of their heads still neatly divided pompadour from pageboy. Dribbles of brown water slid from their victory-rubber boots onto the dark tile floor as they surveyed the room. "See a place?"

Mixed voices rose and fell over the clink of silverware and glass—noise overlaid with smooth, sweet swing flowing from the jukebox, horn notes as neatly clipped and in place as a G.I. haircut.

The men of the U.S. Army Air Corps colored the room olive drab; the bright dots were hairbows and skirts and an occasional civilian necktie. Savory smells of hamburger and onions and fresh-baked apple pie drifted from booths. Up front a veil of smoke hovered over tables weighted with Schlitz and Pabst Blue Ribbon.

The girls spotted a couple leaving a booth, and hurried to claim the space.

The waitress stacked the dishes and pushed them to one side as with her other hand she wiped the dark, varnished tabletop, and with a last quick move, emptied the ashtray onto the saucer that topped the stack. "Be right with you," she called back as she walked toward the kitchen. The girls slid into the booth, facing each other.

Bonnie pulled her arms out of the muskrat coat and arranged it behind her, stuffing gloves into the pockets. "I filed all day. Mr. Forbes was out of town."

Laying back her coat, Maxine regarded her distorted reflection in the chrome napkin holder. "I noticed you weren't at your desk," she said as she unpinned her hat and smoothed her curly blond hair. "What about Alice Faye settling for Don Ameche? I'd have waited for Tyrone Power any day."

Bonnie shrugged. "Maxine, if only we had such a problem!"

As she spoke Bonnie looked around the room, carefully avoiding direct eye contact. Many of the men wore the dark green coats of army officers with one gold bar mounted on each shoulder and new silver wings pinned on their chests. From across the room they looked alike—youthful, lithe bodies, close-cropped hair, uniforms.

Three lieutenants sat together not far from the jukebox, and Bonnie found herself watching the flowing gestures of the dark-haired one in the center who was doing most of the talking. *Good hands. Maybe a doctor.* She tried to put him in a white coat, but it was hard. He looked so good in the uniform. His right hand suddenly became a fist and landed hard on the table. She jumped, then felt relieved when she saw them all laughing. She was glad he wasn't angry, and sorry to have missed the joke.

"Evening, girls."

A soldier leaned over their booth and gripped the table edge, swaying slightly until he found his balance. He was a small man, lean and wiry, with weathered, leathery skin like a farmer. He wore the stripes of a buck sergeant, and gunner wings.

"Excuse me," he continued. "I saw you ladies come in and I just had to talk to you. May I?" He gestured toward Bonnie's bench and, before she could answer, slid around to a tentative perch close to the end. Bonnie sat up and opened her mouth.

He threw up his hands. "My intentions are honorable. So help me God, I gotta tell you that what I want most in the world right now is to ask you to marry me." His face was drawn, his eyes serious.

Bonnie drew back. "Oh come on, soldier," she said weakly, "you've just had too many beers."

"You're right," he said. "Nothing like a few beers to build up a fella's nerve. And that guy's really got his, you're thinking. Fact is, I'm shipping out in a couple of days and in this whole world there ain't one goddamned soul—excuse me, ladies— that's gonna miss me." The little lines around his eyes tightened. "Not a goddamned soul, not a goddamned one."

Bonnie's irritation melted and flowed away.

The sergeant put his elbow on the table and leaned his chin on his hand. "God, you're pretty," he said, his gaze gliding across Bonnie's shiny brown hair. "Goddamn, you're a pretty one."

She reconnoitered. "You've probably got a wife and three kids somewhere. You're just lonely tonight."

"No, ma'am," came the sober answer. "I've got nobody. Not a goddamned soul." He looked down. "I'm a jockey. Hell of a lot rather be riding the tail of a good horse than the tail of a B-26."

"Don't you have any folks?"

"Haven't heard from my family in years. Little late to be looking them up now."

"I'm sorry," she said.

"Hell, I don't want you being sorry," he said, drawing himself up. "It seemed like a good idea at the time."

Bonnie slowly shook her head.

"Five thousand dollars in insurance, and pretty good odds. I'm not a big guy, but I'm a real terror in the backseat of a car."

"No."

The sergeant grinned and rose to his feet. For the first time he looked at Maxine. He gave a lazy wink. "How about you, sweetheart? Like to come over to my table and let me tell you about the ponies?"

"Sorry."

The smile lingered about his thin lips as it died in his eyes. "You're good kids," he said. "Don't worry about it."

Bonnie, watching his retreating back, shook her head. "I wonder what he would have done if I had said yes."

"Taken him a wife I guess, if he hadn't sobered up too soon." Maxine opened her purse and took out a cigarette which she held, unlit. "He was probably just making a pass."

"If you're going to die, even a pass is important."

"They won't all die. Most of them'll come back."

"They have to kill people. Could you kill someone?"

"I don't think so."

"Not even Hitler?"

Maxine shuddered. "Don't ask me. I'm just glad I don't have to. Glad I'm not a man."

"They're doing it for us. And for our children."

"Do you think they'll change? After they kill somebody? Or is it easier for men?"

"I don't think it's easy for anyone."

Maxine took a lighter from her purse and lit the cigarette. "So you're back to those again."

"Yeah." Maxine stared at the smoke. "No reason not to now."

"You heard from Jim?"

"Just a note, sending his new address. I've lost him, Bonnie. I'll never see him again."

"You're not sure."

"He changed when I told him about Janie. He left so soon, wouldn't talk about it."

"You shouldn't have sprung it on him at the last minute."

"How do I handle it, Bonnie? Tell every guy I dance with at the U.S.O. that I'm twenty-one, a stenographer, and incidentally have a four-year-old daughter living back on the farm? It just doesn't fit into the conversation."

"Surely he didn't hold Janie against you?"

"I think it bothered him that I'd been married, that I'd belonged to somebody."

Bonnie frowned. "What gives him the right? He's been around."

"I don't know. Men can't tell you how they feel. I know he likes girls who are feminine—and I liked being feminine for him—even tossing the cigarettes."

"Well, for Pete's sake," Bonnie asked, "what's more feminine than motherhood?"

Maxine shook her head and looked down at her hands. A tear sparkled on her lashes.

Their waitress sidestepped a grope as she came back for their order, and Bonnie and Maxine asked for coffee.

As the waitress turned, a man's hand touched her drooping shoulders, a handsome gold watch showing from beneath a wool sleeve. Looking above wide shoulders, Bonnie contacted blue eyes that looked into hers and held. She recognized the dark-haired lieutenant she had been watching earlier.

"Excuse me." His voice was pleasant and low, a clipped accent separating the words. "Before you order, how about considering the case of three lonely soldiers. It's two long hours till curfew." He turned back to the waitress and smiled as he asked, "Can you take the order at our table—that is, if these ladies will join us?"

The waitress straightened her apron and fluttered her hand across the crooked hair net. He turned back to Maxine and then to Bonnie. "I'm John," he said.

Bonnie heard a distant voice saying, "I'm Maxine."

If we had gone straight home tonight this wouldn't be happening. He has been watching me. He saw me reject the sergeant. She said, "I'm sorry; we really should be going."

Maxine frowned and squirmed.

Placing both hands on the table edge, John leaned down. She strained to catch his words. "Please come. Just for a beer. We won't even ask your last names. A month from now you won't remember, but we will."

I'll remember. I'll remember. "We really shouldn't, but—"

John straightened up and reached for Bonnie's coat.

"That's not my table," the waitress said. She looked tired again.

"Thank you, you've been very helpful," Bonnie said. She felt a ridiculous impulse to embrace the girl.

John folded her coat across his arm. The fur clung to the wool uniform, filling in the spaces between his arm and body. Bonnie slid from the booth into the aisle. Their eyes met and turned away.

Maxine pulled her coat about her shoulders and, chatting comfortably, picked up her hat. Bonnie heard not a word.

Crossing near the jukebox, they sidestepped a dancing couple. "What did you say you did before you got drafted?" she heard the girl ask as they glided by.

"It's the first table," John said.

The two men pushed back their chairs and stood up. The blond, stocky one crushed his cigarette in the overflowing tray and smiled. He lifted his hand toward his wings, dropping it suddenly to grab a chair, which he pulled out for Maxine. John introduced him as Joe and the other man as Ed. Ed's movements were as slow and connected as Joe's were spasmodic. He stood quietly, resting the weight of his lean body on one leg. Bonnie felt his eyes sliding over her, touching her, yet the irritation his appraisal aroused in her was laced with pleasure. She slid into the shaky bentwood chair and crossed her legs. John moved in beside her.

"Y'all got a friendly town here," Joe said, "—for the guys from the base."

Maxine took a long last look at John and turned to Joe with a flash of even teeth. "What part of the South are you from?" she asked.

John angled his shoulder away from the other couple, his gaze pulling Bonnie aside, speeding her heartbeat, stealing her breath. "And what do you do?" he asked.

"Guess."

He pretended to think. "Librarian. No—teacher. Nurse. A caring person. There's a softness. . . ."

"I'm a secretary—in our biggest defense plant."

His head bobbed slowly. "Efficient, no misspelled words. Files at your fingertips. Brewing hot coffee for the boss, and remembering his wife's birthday."

"He doesn't have a wife."

"Well, if he did you'd remember her birthday."

"Maybe. I have other responsibilities."

Their eyes, which had been constantly connecting and disengaging, came together again as he said, "I'm sorry. I would expect you to. You have intelligent eyes."

No one had ever told her she had intelligent eyes before.

"What do they build at your plant?"

"Airplane parts. Hardware. Bolts and screws."

Ed caught her reply. "Hey," he crowed, "you work in a screw factory."

"You could say so," she answered, forcing a smile.

"It all helps to win the war," John said.

"Sure, for want of a screw the war could be lost," Joe joined in, a grin tickling the corner of his mouth.

A funny snorting sound came from Ed, and for a moment, they all teetered on the edge of joining him. Bonnie clasped her hands on the table, one thumb sliding along the other. Then, lean, brown fingers closed over her cold ones. "Drop it, Jackson," John said, still looking at Bonnie. "Would you like to dance?"

He took his hand away and she took it back when they came together in front of the jukebox. The other hand slid around her waist, and her head fit into the space between the hollow of his shoulder and his chin. They were one body as the voice crooned, "Speak low, when you speak love." They made the small, smooth movements of the foxtrot on the miniature dance floor.

"All of us are wound up," he said, close to her ear. "Don't hold it against him."

"It's nothing; I've heard it before. Is he a good friend of yours?"

"I just met Joe and Ed. We're crew mates."

We're late, darling, we're late.
The curtain descends, everything ends
too soon, too soon.
I wait, darling, I wait.
Won't you speak low to me, speak love to me
And soon.

She lifted her head. *Crew mates! That meant he was scheduled to leave soon.* He answered her unspoken question.

He said, "About a week."

A whole week. Seven times tonight.

"What are you doing for the next week?" John asked.

"Can't think of a blessed thing."

The record ended, and she looked down, guarding her pleasure.

The slick, quick beat of the swinging "American Patrol" intruded. Jitterbug! His hand moved from her back and quickly grasped her other hand. Without missing a step they fell into the split-second synchronization of Lindy footwork. She twisted and spun on the pivot of his wrist, flew away and back again as his strong arm reversed, the push-and-pull intercourse as intimate as a shared heartbeat. Boy, girl, and beat melted together, indivisible as the nation.

When the music stopped they embraced, wetness mingling where her forehead lay against his chin. The world gradually settled down around them. They had an audience. Someone applauded. Bonnie stepped back.

"Man," she breathed, "you sure can dance."

"Found my partne.," he said.

Two girls stood by the jukebox, figures hidden by outsized cashmere sweaters sagging past their hiplines over pleated plaid skirts that stopped just below their knees. Thick, white socks bunched above their dirty saddle shoes. The girls smiled at John and he smiled back, nodding.

"College girls!" Bonnie said.

John grinned, and looked back over his shoulder after they passed.

"Go ahead, ask them to dance."

"They're just babies."

He took her hand and threaded through the tables.

When they were seated, she said, "I'll bet you're a college man. Ivy League."

"Why do you say that?"

"Aren't you?"

"Harvard, class of '42. How could you tell?"

"You look like a Harvard man."

"Known a lot of Harvard men?"

"Nope. You're the first. But you look like one."

"I've expected to be a Harvard lawyer ever since I can remember."

"You will be."

"Maybe. Didn't plan to take to the air, but here I am."

"The war has improved my life, tripled my salary. Bought me a muskrat."

"Did you go to the state university here?"

"No, I went to junior college in my home town. Came to Lancaster to work. It's just a little place, my home town."

Across the table Ed stood up and reached for his coat. "If you folks can manage without me, I think I'll cruise."

Bonnie said, "We didn't mean to leave you out."

"That's all right, honey. There's bound to be something stirring around here. They can't all be nice girls."

"Don't you like nice girls?"

"They're okay when you've got the time." He stood holding the coat like a sad child. "See you guys at the bus."

Bonnie and John watched him walk with a little restless

bounce through the congested room. He slowed once as he eyed a girl with curly red hair sitting in the far corner. The girl looked at him, but she was not alone, and Ed put on his coat and went out the door.

John leaned back in his chair. "Just think, an hour ago I didn't know I'd be sitting here with you."

"A development not entirely out of your control."

He grinned and cocked his head. "Well, maybe I give fate a little push now and then, but I don't give her any trouble when she pushes back."

"Does it really matter that it's me? Wouldn't any other girl have done just as well?"

"Maybe, we don't know yet, do we? Why are you with me instead of with the sergeant or Ed or the captain over there?"

"Guess I'm swinging with the surprises, too."

"This has happened to you before."

She lifted a hand. "The rules have changed."

"Of course. We've already established that you're a nice girl."

"How do you tell? How do guys decide?"

"Interesting question, we'll look into it. I want to see you again."

"I'm glad."

"Are you waiting for someone?"

"No. Is there someone waiting?"

"No commitments. There is a girl in Boston I've known all my life." He leaned forward. "Know what?"

Her face grew warm. "What?"

"I don't know your name."

They shared quick laughter, reliving the intimacy of the dance. She told him her name.

From the end of the table Maxine called "Bonnie," and pointed toward the wide door leading to the hotel lobby. Their little sergeant and a tall woman headed for the door. He encircled her waist with his arm, and tried to match his steps to hers as she teetered on three-inch heels. She pulled away from him and bent down to remove the shoes. They seemed to be laughing over the improvement this made in their coupling, and she proceeded toward the lobby in her stocking feet, the sergeant sauntering close behind.

John murmured into Bonnie's ear, "Lose some, win some."

Two

Bonnie and John met for steaks and a movie on Saturday night with Joe and Maxine. On Sunday afternoon, bundled against the cold, the two of them explored downtown Lancaster, window-shopping at Murray and Penn's, walking the paths of the university campus, and arriving at the capitol building in time for a tour. They talked tirelessly, comparing and contrasting their lives and their dreams. Their fathers both had fought in World War I. His mother went to finishing school, hers hadn't finished high school. Her grandparents were farmers, his were sailors and city landlords. They both liked Tchaikovsky, Clark Gable, and rhubarb pie. Also school, October, and Richard Halliburton.

At the bowling alley they stopped in the lounge for a cup of hot chocolate and decided to try a few lines. John was good; she was glad she didn't have to let him win.

Bonnie poised the heavy ball in front of her, swung it back and forward again during three measured steps, then let go out of a graceful swing, knees bent. John watched with approval as her tweed skirt flared and dipped over the old shoes she usually left inside her boots.

Most of the alleys were empty on this gloomy Sunday afternoon. At the end of the lane, the pin boy scrambled to reset the pins and to climb back to his perch above them.

"No matter how well we knock them down, he just keeps putting them back," John remarked.

"Like recovering from the wars."

"Suppose we'll find the weapon from which we can't recover?"

"Were you a pacifist in high school?" she asked.

"God yes, weren't we all? I once took the Oxford Pledge."

She tried to remember what that was.

"A pledge some students took refusing to support the United States in any war."

"I think I read about it."

"The radical peace movements were breaking down by the time I got to college. I joined the American Student Union when it was on its last legs. The Communist faction sabotaged the anti-war program, and the pacifists pulled out."

He spoke of these things as though they were real—these things you read about, idealized, but didn't do.

He finished, "We thought we had the simple answers. But life isn't simple."

"No. Look at you now."

John adjusted his fingers inside the holes in the ball and lifted it from the rack. "See the number one pin?" he said. "That's der Fuehrer."

His arm swung back. The black ball connected with the alley and spun ahead. The pin setter scurried to safety before the triangle of pins exploded, their perfect order fragmented into chaos.

Back in boots, knitted white stocking cap, and trailing scarf, Bonnie strolled with John toward her apartment at dusk. They walked, eyes lowered, watching the sidewalk for slick spots. They cut through the park, strolling under trees and past bushes heavy with ice. They stopped to rest at a concrete picnic area, sitting on the cold bench and leaning back against the table.

"I'll bet you forgot the watermelon," John said.

"Thought you were bringing it," she answered.

"It had to stay in the Frigidaire as long as possible. One

hundred in the shade today." He placed a gloved hand over her mitten on the bench between them. "I never could stand the heat. Think of me when you share the melon with some other soldier next summer."

"Can't kid me," she whispered because he was coming closer. "There isn't any next summer."

Their first kiss barely touched, fragile, a small spark in a freezing night. "Yes there is, Bonnie. That's the way it works." He kissed her again. "Hot and cold."

She stood up, stepped onto the dead grass, the frosted blades crackling under her boots. John sat on the bench watching, then followed. He matched her slow steps. "What's the matter?"

She shook her head. They stopped and looked back at the cold, white picnic table, silent and empty.

"It looks like a statue," John said.

She shivered. "It looks like a tomb."

"It was alive when we were there."

"Were we ever there?"

"Yes, Bonnie. We were. Don't forget."

She turned to face him and slid both hands up the lapels of his overcoat and under his upturned collar. They leaned together and through layers of heavy clothing she felt him against her. Flesh found flesh as warm mouths and cold noses touched and lingered.

Bonnie strained to control her trembling.

"You're cold, darling," he whispered.

He kept a protective arm about her shoulders as they turned to walk back to her apartment.

That night, in a room lighted only by the glow of the fireplace grate, his hand sliding down her bare arm, gently touching a cheek before a kiss, resting upon a wool-skirted thigh, cradling an uncovered breast, stirred excitement she hadn't dared dream of. In past experience, touching had set off alarms, produced shields. Tonight touching opened doors through which she dared not—would not—pass.

Three

By Tuesday, they were old friends, sweethearts. After work Bonnie hurried home to change into something loose and soft. She left off her brassiere, but after reapplying lipstick she unzipped and put it back on.

She knew his knock. It was a sound she would always be able to recall. John brought records—Ravel, Prokofiev and Scho³nberg, a new kind of music.

The new music became a part of the new life. In years to come, its sound would resurrect in memory one special week when the warm walls of a lamplit apartment closed out winter. Shared suppers in the little kitchenette were communion for two. Less than perfect sound from the portable phonograph was a background for the eager flow of words. Words gave way to silent listening as they held each other in the dark, on the mohair sofa, knowing consummation was out of reach.

The night John brought the records they moved to the sofa with cheese and apples after they finished the stew, leaving the scraped, stacked dishes in the sink. Cheese for dessert was new for Bonnie. They did this in Boston.

John readjusted the records on the changer. The stack would play through quickly, another heavy record dropping after each piece ended.

"Are you playing the Ravel waltzes again?" Bonnie asked. "So beautiful. I only knew 'Bolero' before."

She sat on one foot on the sofa after kicking off her shoes. John dropped into the slip-covered easy chair. He leaned forward, elbows balanced on spread knees. "No, I saved those for last. This album is Schönberg. Know his music?"

Bonnie shook her head. "Never heard of him. My school was strictly Bach, Beethoven and Brahms. Oh my, that is strange."

Rhythm changed without pattern. Melodies leaped and chords were random, chaotic.

"What's the matter, pet?"

"Never heard anything like that before." She put both feet on the floor.

"A lot of artists were trying to get rid of the rules about the time he was composing. Some of the music can't even be written on a conventional staff."

They watched the record spinning on the phonograph.

"I had—have—a friend who writes this kind of music," John said. "I used to listen with him. He signed the pledge with me in 1938, but right after Pearl Harbor he went out and enlisted. Now he's missing in action.

"He joined the young Communists after the American Student Union. We sometimes talked about it far into the night.

"I went to some of the meetings, but couldn't ever quite bring myself to join."

"This girl of yours in Boston, I'll bet she likes this music."

John looked up. "Yes, she does." He shook his head. "Do you know how often you pick up my thoughts?"

"You were thinking about her?"

"Well, yes. She was with Eric and me sometimes." He inspected the toe of his shoe. "I suspected Sara liked him quite a lot, but he didn't care for girls. Just music."

"He probably figured she was your girl."

"What?"

"You said she liked Eric but he didn't like her."

"I didn't say that."

"Yes you did. You said she liked Eric but he didn't care for—"

She stopped as he moved to the sofa, and took hold of her upper arm. He kissed her lightly. "We all grew up together."

The insistent, dissonant chords of the record pounded against her temples as a stranger surrounded her with his body. She placed both hands against his chest and pushed. The strong male wall did not yield. In a flutter of panic she pushed harder. He sat back, surprise stirring across his face.

"Turn it off," she said, putting her hands over her ears and closing her eyes. When she opened them he was still there, solemnly watching. She dropped her eyes. "It scares me."

He stood up, walked over and shut off the music. With care he lifted the stack of heavy records off the machine. He laid them on the table and reached for the old records. She heard the needle scratch. The familiar predictable notes of "Liebestraum" lay like a calm mantle over the remembered chaos of Schönberg.

Sliding a pack of Camels from the pocket of his uniform jacket draped over a chair back, John sat down out of reach and concentrated on lighting the cigarette before leaning back to look at her. "This music's nice, too," he said.

The crook of his finger over the cigarette, and the curve of his hand resting on his knee stirred the pit of her stomach. "I'll learn to like the Schönberg," she said. "It's just so new."

"Sure you will."

"I wish I had known Eric."

"I do, too."

"Do you think I'm stupid?"

"No, Bonnie. You're not stupid." He added softly, "The music reaches you; most people can't even hear it. There's something in you, wrapped up in the sweetness, that I want to uncover—if only there was time. I don't want to leave you, Bonnie. I want to know the woman you will be, as you'll come to know her. I never wanted anything so goddamned bad."

Could it be that I am superior? Not only not stupid but superior! How good it is, holding our eyes together and not needing to look away. I feel naked before him and I'm not ashamed. He knows me and I know he's supposed to. She lifted her arm and stretched her hand toward him.

John walked over to change the record. "Clair de Lune" had been repeating for twenty minutes. He switched the machine off and stood with his back to her. The light from the street sliced through the venetian blind, casting diagonal lines across the rug.

"How long does it take to get married here?" he asked.

Sitting in the dark, Bonnie's hand went to her throat.

He spun around and she jumped. "I mean, is there a waiting period? How long?"

It wasn't the right question, but she followed his lead. "Three days."

"Tomorrow's Wednesday. I could get a weekend pass. Can't be sure, but it looks like we'll be here till next week." He took a step, then faltered. "God A'mighty, it would be a dumb thing to do!"

He walked over and switched on the lamp. He was restored to her sight, as exciting as the feel of him in the dark. Bonnie straightened and put her hands to her hair.

John's thoughtful gaze moved from her to the muted landscape print hanging above the sofa, to the crushed, petal-dotted pillows at the end, down to the worn leather footstool, over the untouched plate of cheese on the table, and back to her.

"Well, when you make up your mind, let me know." Bonnie's nervous laugh slid into a hiccup.

"Let's do it," he said. "Let's be idiots and do it."

He sat down and grasped her hands, suddenly reversing himself to stand again and pace. "Could you get to a doctor tomorrow for the blood test? I can get mine at the base. You'll need to see the doctor for something else, too. Are diaphragms legal in this state? You know they—"

"I *know* what they are!" Her cheeks warmed.

He sat down again and touched one hand. "Oh, sweetheart," he asked, "Is it okay? Do you want to?"

And she said, "Yes."

Four

When they came into the apartment the next night, they walked slowly and hung up their coats without speaking. The marriage license they had just applied for made them a different combination. She stood in the doorway, staring at the stove when John came up behind her.

"I like my steak rare, and lots of onion in the meat loaf," he said, reading her mind again.

"It's a gamble, isn't it, for a man," she said. "Taking on a cook for the rest of his life without asking for references. I think I'll just open some cans."

"It doesn't matter what we eat," John answered, seating himself on a high stool. "I'm not hungry, I just wanted to see you in the kitchen tonight—talk to you over our own table. I want to remember you in as many ways as possible. You can't believe all the questions that run through my mind when I'm trying to get to sleep."

"For instance?"

"Well, let's see. How about high school? Were you a prom queen or a cheerleader?"

Could she tell him she didn't have a steady boyfriend until after high school? She answered truthfully, "Neither, I'm afraid. I was class valedictorian, and I had the lead in the senior class play."

"Sweet, untarnished, beautiful, and bright. You'll make those brittle, wiseacre debutantes look like dull brass next to simple, pure gold.

"Maybe we'll go to school together after the war. You could finish up your degree while I'm in law school. It would mean putting off a family for a while."

She started stirring again. "I don't think a couple should have children right away. They need to get used to each other."

"We'll need to, for sure." He jumped off the stool. "You're boiling over!"

She switched off the burner, and turned her attention to getting the haphazard supper on the table. Once seated, they could back to what was important. "Speaking of children—" she said.

"Another thing we haven't covered. How many? What do you think?"

"Two," she answered promptly. "A boy and a girl."

"Yeah. Okay. Maybe even three or four wouldn't be bad. You were an only child, and my brother didn't come along until I was ten. I think we missed something."

"Two's enough. About three years apart."

John put down his fork and reached across and covered her hand. "It gives me something to think about, plans to make. Something to live for."

The food she was chewing turned to a soggy lump. She swallowed it, feeling its push all the way down. John slid back his chair and walked around the table. She kept looking at him until he pulled her gently to her feet and began kissing her. She welcomed the kisses, and returned them with love spilling over.

They moved to the sofa, and he unbuttoned her blouse and pushed up her brassiere, touching and kissing her breasts for the first time with the lights on. She was fascinated to watch his long fingers cup the little mounds, and wondered how he knew to brush the nipples so lightly instead of squeezing and hurting as had happened to her before. The sight of his moving hands excited her, made things happen lower, under her skirt. John loosened his tie and top shirt buttons and undid her bra in the back. She was passive at first, but discovered that her enjoyment increased when she felt his ear, or stroked the stubbly hair above it, or slid her hand into his shirt and found hair again—soft and curly on his chest. They continued to kiss and stroke, and occasionally to talk, until it was time for him to leave. They never touched, or disturbed their clothing, below the waist.

She left work early on Thursday, telling Mr. Forbes she was having an out-of-town guest. She splurged on a taxi and bought groceries. They planned to stay in the apartment for their weekend honeymoon, but each day had to count for itself. She felt uneasy about sending him away hungry last night.
She considered meat loaf but was afraid it might not be as

good as his mother's recipe, and settled for a thick steak to be baked with mushrooms and served with mashed potatoes and gravy. She used a bright blue tablecloth with multicolored pottery dishes, and bought a new white candle for the clear glass holder, but put it away in favor of a short candle with a blackened wick and dribbled wax streaking its sides and squeezed it into a squatty green wine bottle. She wore the pink housecoat. This time she left off the brassiere. She balanced the Ravel records on the spindle of the record changer so they could be switched on when the knock came.

Rummaging through stacks of notebook paper in the closet, she set aside certain segments, to be taken into the living room and stacked on the table by the sofa.

She expected him around six—shortly after the time she usually got home. When the knock came she flew to start the record player, then to the door, stopping in front of it to take a deep breath and smooth her hair. It could be fun, getting ready for your man to come home.

When John came inside, he stopped short. "Hey now," he exclaimed, "Hey, look at this."

She smiled and put her arm around his waist. "Surprise," she said, "I got off early."

Warm, soft arcs of light radiated from the candle, lamp, and fireplace. Thinking of the chasm of time that separated them from a lifetime of such homecomings made her ache inside.

When she went to finish dinner, she pointed to the piles of paper on the table. "The story I told you about, and some poems. Thought you might like to look at them."

He hurried to settle himself. She stopped talking while he read, turning the pages quickly; but she glanced at him often, trying to interpret the expression on his face. The gravy became lumpy, and she poured it into the bowl through a large, misshapen tea strainer. Thirty minutes later she called him. Dinner was cooling off.

"Well?" she asked when they were settled.

"It's delicious," he pronounced, finishing the first taste.

"No, no, I mean the story. What do you think?"

He looked thoughtful while chewing, then swallowed and said, "It's good, Bonnie, very good."

She shook her head. "You didn't like it."

"Yes I did, I liked it. You have talent, I really mean that. You should keep writing."

"But—?"

"Well, it takes a long time, a lot of work. The talent is just the beginning."

"I've been writing since second grade."

"I'm sure you have, it shows. You should major in English," he said as they ate. "Why'd you set your story in New York?"

"I don't know. It's kind of a fairy-tale place to me. It was fun to imagine—"

"Haven't you ever been there?"

"No. I suppose you have."

"Sure, often. It's close to home."

She went back for the coffee. She was always forgetting to pour the coffee.

"Why don't you write a story about Lancaster? About things happening to you?"

She poured and sat down. "I've thought about it," she said. "Maybe it's too close."

"Someday you must. Life in a midwestern army air base town during the great war."

"I do write a lot of letters." It occurred to her that that would soon change. "But I'll have to stop, won't I? Write and tell them I'm married."

"Maybe not. Letters are so important to a soldier."

"You don't mind my writing to other men?"

"Maybe I will mind at that, though it seems selfish."

"It's not selfish; we'll be forsaking all others."

"Yes, of course."

"Is the steak all right?" she asked anxiously.

He had told her he liked his steak rare, and she had served it baked, well-done.

"It's delicious," he said again.

After the dishes were stacked they sat down together surrounded by the well-thumbed papers accumulated from childhood, through adolescence, into the early bloom of maturity.

"Don't stop writing," John told her. "Don't let me or the kids stop you. I may try, you know."

"I've so much to learn. You're ahead of me, but it's what I want. Help me, John, take me with you."

"I will, Bonnie, I will. I want to."

He hugged her and she clung to him. All their plans were fantasies, shining on the other side of a canyon of separation and death.

"You talked about communism," she spoke from the sanctity of his chest. "It's very foreign to me. I didn't know Americans ever thought about it."

They moved apart.

"There's been so much suffering," John said. "People who can't find work going hungry and cold or being humiliated by going on relief. I thought about that for a long time. Why *not* divide up the jobs and divide up the money?"

"Simple answers again."

"Exactly. I wanted simple answers when I was eighteen. But there's a price to pay. The sacrifice of freedom and dreams, the very things America was built on. There has to be another way."

"Hasn't the war given people jobs?"

"We may have more prosperity than we've ever known when it's over, but first we have to survive."

"Everybody wants to survive," she said. "The war brings us together."

"And tears us apart," he remembered, returning to the personal.

Bonnie went to the phonograph and started a record. "You'd Be So Nice to Come Home To," a male voice crooned.

"Good choice," he commented.

"It's the kind of song they're writing these days," she told him.

A song of separation. Bonnie listened and followed the beat.

Five

He hadn't telephoned her at work before. On Friday morning he said "Bonnie?" like somebody died. "Bad news, sweetheart."

She forced sound from her dry throat. "What?" The fluorescent light across the aisle flickered. It made her dizzy.

"Our orders came. We're shipping out tomorrow morning."

Sue, the mail girl, dropped some papers into Bonnie's "In" box. Sue waited. When Bonnie looked up at her she went on, mumbling something Bonnie didn't hear.

"I'm sorry," he was saying.

"We can't get married?"

"I'm confined to quarters."

What's the matter with the maintenance men around here! I asked to have that light fixed two days ago. Or was it Monday? "This is it? On the phone?"

"Listen, I'll call you tonight. We'll have a long talk."

"Tonight."

"I know you can't talk now, but I wanted you to know. You may need to cancel some things."

"Yes. I will." *Not much trouble. The arrangements aren't complicated. Not like the wedding I might have had. "I Love You Truly" and "Oh Promise Me."*

"I'm so sorry."

"Oh, John, so am I."

"I love you, darling. I always will, remember that."

"I'll remember."

She hung up the phone. *The decision wasn't ours. Life will stay the same. No, it won't. I'll wait. Ask me to wait. That other girl is waiting. Without commitment. I'll be committed. Ask me. Come back to me. Just come back. So many good-byes. Even the ones who say "I love you" stop writing. This time I said it back. This one is different. This one is a two-way street. Come back to me. Come back. Come back. Lord, make him come back. John.*

"Is Mr. Forbes in?"

"No, he went to a meeting."

"When will he be back?"

Not for the duration. Maybe never. "What?"

"When will he be back? Bonnie, is something wrong?"

"No. What did you say? Oh, he'll be back around noon, I guess."

"You don't look so good. Too many late hours?" He winked.

"No, it's that light. It makes me dizzy."

She didn't hear the car pool conversation. Clouds hung low and damp cold crept into the car. A long talk with Maxine had helped. Maxine, Joe, and Bonnie's pastor were the only ones who knew about the wedding planned for tomorrow. She and John had decided to brave the storm of parental disapproval after the fact. Parents wouldn't understand that you could be sure in a week.

Her feet were heavy on the stairs. She hurried around the landing. He sat on the top step, her lieutenant. Ankles crossed, knees spread, his short topcoat rested over them. His flight cap was pushed to the back of his head, exposing short, dark bristles of hair. He was up in one movement to lift her off her feet and swing her around to the door.

She couldn't stop hugging him. "Oh, I'm so glad you're here."

He pushed her gently back. "The key."

She dug in the bottom of her purse, mindless rummaging that finally produced a key. They moved inside.

"I had to come. Even AWOL."

She shut the door. "You're not!"

"It's okay, the army doesn't know. It's our secret."

"Are you sure?"

"No problem at the gate, my buddies'll cover in the squad room, but I have to catch the bus before curfew. We take off at eight in the morning."

Her smile faded. "Oh. For a minute, I thought—"

"Bonnie," his voice lowered, "I can't make the date we had for tomorrow. But we're all ready. It's still six and a half hours to midnight. Do you think your preacher—?"

"Oh, glory," she said. She dashed to the phone, flinging her hat and gloves aside as she ran. She struggled with boots with one hand as she held the phone with the other. After a brief conversation she turned a glowing face back to John. "He'll meet us at the church chapel in an hour."

"Great." He grinned as she waltzed about the room in her stocking feet, still wearing her bulky wool coat.

"We can come back here." She looked about the apartment, in shining readiness for tomorrow's postnuptial celebration for four. "We'll drink the champagne by ourselves."

"Bonnie," he extended a hand and pulled her toward the window. "Look out there." They saw a bleak landscape, already sinking into night. The lights in the window of the house across the street framed a fine spray of freezing rain.

"I want in the worst way to come back here, but don't you think we should stay down at the hotel? Close to the church and the terminal?"

She shook her head. "This is our place; I want you to remember."

"It'd save a lot of time. As it is, we'll have to depend on the bus. Wouldn't want to try for a cab in this weather."

"The weather! You can't fly in this weather!"

His face did not reflect her excitement. "It won't make any difference for us. It could clear tonight. Even if it doesn't I have to go back—to stick around."

She closed her eyes. "So stupid of me to keep looking for a reprieve."

They stood holding hands, looking out at the cold, empty street.

"I wonder if it will be warmer where I am next week?" John squeezed her fingers.

She gasped. "You know! You have your orders! Where?"

"It's a military secret."

"Don't tease." She pulled his hand up and clasped it. "You know I won't tell."

He lifted her hands to his lips and kissed her fingertips. "Let's just say it's good I prefer plum pudding over coconuts."

She let out a long breath. "Oh, that's good. Yes, good—it's not the Pacific."

He nodded. "It's the assignment we wanted." He pulled her toward him. She resisted gently and freed her hands.

"I have to dress," she told him in a low voice. "I want to wear my wedding dress. It's important, isn't it?"

He didn't answer, and she walked toward the bedroom, adding over her shoulder, "Turn on some lights and start the fireplace grate if you're cold. I'll hurry."

Her hand was on the knob when he called her name again. She stopped without turning around.

"Bonnie, could I come in? I won't slow you down, won't touch you."

She turned slowly. His head was outlined against the window, face in shadow.

"I won't be here tomorrow to watch you dress—Lord knows when we'll be together again."

"I—I'd rather not." She forced herself to look at him. He nodded. She went through the door and shut it.

She hurried to bathe and dress. Two walls of guilt pressed in. Had she appeased the right one? She must make it up to him. He wouldn't have long to wait.

When she emerged from the steamy bathroom, she was reassured by the light shining under the door and the sound of the radio. The nasal voice of H. V. Kaltenborn came through clearly, bringing the evening news. "R.A.F. and American bombers continue their relentless pounding of military targets in Germany. Allied losses were somewhat lighter this week."

Reaching for the short, white wool dress, she stopped and grasped the closet doorjamb. She leaned her hand against it, shuddering. She wanted to scream and weep. She wanted to throw open the door. Instead, she dressed faster, and packed a small bag with her high-heeled white satin pumps and her new peignoir and nightdress, tucking the bulky prescription box underneath.

Her work clothes and coat lay heaped on the white counterpane. She took the muskrat from the closet and laid it across her arm, picked up the bag and walked in her stocking feet to the door.

John had switched off the radio when the station reverted to music and was standing before the fireplace, head lowered, hands in pockets. The fire made a yellow glow on the rug, and brass buttons and silver wings glistened in reflected light. *Dear John.*

He turned around. *See me. Remember. I'm part of you, making you whole. Tied to you, pulling you back. The real life. The good part. Your bride.*

"Do you like my dress?"

"You're beautiful."

She sighed. Spotting the boots, crossing each other on the floor by the sofa, she sat down and pulled out a dusty shoe and put it on.

"Bonnie?"

"Ummmmm?"

"It's hard to talk about."

"I know."

"I mean what I've been thinking. I don't know why I didn't think about it before."

She straightened and put the foot on the floor. "What?"

"It's what I'm doing to you."

"Doing to me?"

He walked closer. "I've been looking out only for myself. Wanting to keep everything the same until I could come back and finish it."

"So?"

"Have you thought how it's going to be for you in the meantime? I know how you are. You'll wait."

"Of course I'll wait. That's what I want to do. Wait."

"But can you just put your life on hold? It could be years."

"Isn't that what *you're* doing?"

She was sorry about the waves in her voice. He was standing over her; she had to look up. "John, what are you trying to say?"

"Whatever it is, I seem to be saying it badly." He started to lean over, then straightened. "Bonnie, are you very sure that you want to be married? Have you really thought what it means?"

"I don't know what *you* mean. I won't be any different from all the other wives. It's what women do."

He shook his head. "We've understood each other so well. I don't know why now—"

"All right. Tell me. Do you want out?"

He drew in his breath.

"Because if you do, you can say so. You don't have to make it sound like you're doing it for me."

He sat down beside her. "Okay, okay. I'm sorry I mentioned it, please forget that I did."

She saw him through blurred eyes.

"Forgive me?"

She nodded.

"Of course," he said, "I really was thinking of you."

She gave him a long look before asking quietly, "What would be the alternative?"

His face drew tight. He stood and raised his voice. "I don't know. It's not as though I were making plans." He sat down again. "I'm trying to be realistic. Maybe it's just everyday pre-wedding jitters."

"This isn't an everyday wedding. You already said it's a dumb thing to do."

A freshly starched yellow linen cloth covered the little table where they ate. The square phonograph with its stack of records sat waiting. This room was their whole life together. Outside, the sleet hit the window in uneven gasps.

She forced her eyes to move from her own hands to his face. "Do you want to marry me without a wedding? Then we wouldn't be committed, we'd still be free." She watched several answers cross his face.

"That would be an intelligent approach, if we could handle it."

She steadied her chin. "I'll do it any way you want, John," she said at last. *It won't make any difference to me. I'm committed.*

This was the moment for him to reach out for her, but a wall stood between them, as solid as it was invisible.

John sighed and stood up. He looked down at her feet, one shoe on and one shoe off. He bent on one knee and pulled the shoe out of the other boot. Grasping her heel, he guided her foot into the shoe. He then lifted the boots one at a time and together they tugged them on over her shoes.

"Please get up off your knees," she said. "I feel silly."

He laid one hand on the sofa arm as he regained his feet, then reached out his arms and pulled her up. Their hands passed on around each other and they held on, fingers spread, his face pressing into her hair. They separated and he picked up her coat.

At the door Bonnie said "Oh," and ran back to the refrigerator for the bottle of champagne, placing it in a paper bag and hurrying back. John put it in his pocket, but the bottle bulged and extended out too far.

Bonnie opened her suitcase and laid the tall bottle across the wispy blue peignoir, and snapped the case shut. John paused in the doorway, but without looking back, he pulled the door shut behind them.

Six

A mantle of crystal had settled over the city. Freezing mist veiled the near and obscured the distant. Winter twilight vanquished color. Diamond trees lined platinum streets. The sidewalk stretched into a flat ribbon of ice.

Noise would shatter the brittle air. She whispered, "Beautiful. Oh, it's beautiful."

John dropped the suitcase. He rounded the end of the sidewalk with a few steps. Bonnie's squeal violated the silence as, arms spread for banking, he slid down the declining walk parallel to the street, skillfully guiding himself onto the grass at the bottom of the incline.

She shrieked again and laughed. "You're crazy—going the wrong way."

"Who's crazy?" he shouted. "You can't slide uphill."

She took a few cautious steps to the turn in the sidewalk and spread out her arms. "Catch me. Here I come."

Her jerky running start turned into a lurching slalom. The boots weren't made for sliding but she managed to keep upright all the way down into John's outstretched arms.

Without consultation, they climbed up the frozen grass and slid down the walk again together.

"Shall we press our luck?" he panted.

"Why not?"

This time they almost didn't make it, Bonnie clutching wildly at his steady, strong arm. Their gasps exploded into laughter, bouncing into a picture postcard world.

"If you think that's good, wait till we put on our skates," John said.

They climbed back up the incline and she waited for him to retrieve her bag before they threaded their way across the grass in the other direction.

"You'll like our lodge in the Adirondacks. Know how to ski?"

She shook her head. "But I can learn."

"You'll be great. I can't wait to teach you."

She looked around. "Think there's anybody else out there?"

He looked carefully, pointing through the haze across the street. "Up in that tree, there's an old man in a pointed cap and cowboy boots. He's the only one."

She stopped and cupped her hands around her mouth. "Hey, old man," she called, "did you know this is my wedding night?"

"I don't think he heard you."

She raised her hands again, shouting, "Hey, old man—"

"I'll help. *Hey*—"

Bonnie pulled back on his arm. "John," she said, "we're lunatics."

"Momma and Poppa Lunatic, talking about a future."

"Oh, tell me there's a future."

"I promise. Thirty years from now you'll be a gentle old lady in a shawl with our grandchildren gathered around you saying, 'Tell me about your wedding during the big war, Granma.' "

She smiled. "And you'll be an old man in a pointed cap and cowboy boots sitting up in a tree spying on lovers."

They were the only passengers on the bus. The diminutive driver kept her attention riveted on the icy pavement, skillfully easing the big vehicle up to stop signs and around corners.

Downtown, the few people on the street eased by like ghosts. Out of the mist the gray stone church loomed like a deserted Gothic castle. They rounded the corner, past the steep stone steps, to see a light shining through the small stained-glass windows of the chapel. Like a candle in the window at home, it drew them to the less imposing side entrance. They held each other up one last time on the stone steps, and stood tall again with firm footing in the dry hallway.

The hall was chilly, but when they passed through the heavy chapel doors, warmer air touched their stiff faces and fingers. Mellowed wood panelled the walls here, and the deep red carpet echoed the somber colors of stained-glass windows

with night on the other side. Light was hushed by the amber
bulbs in the antique chandelier, and the low-flamed candles in
the brass candelabra.

A small man with thinning hair and glasses came toward
them, his hand outstretched to grasp Bonnie's.

"Here you are, my dear. Wretched night out there."

She was grateful for his warm handclasp, and turned to
introduce John. Dr. Miller examined the bridegroom.

"Glad to meet you. I know Bonnie will have chosen a good
man."

"Thank you, sir," John replied.

"We're a little late," Bonnie said. "You'll be late for your
meeting."

Dr. Miller shook his head. "Doesn't matter, they can start
without me. This is more important."

Two persons stood close to the altar. Bonnie recognized the
fuzzy round figure of the church secretary, but she wasn't sure
who the man was.

They left their coats and the leather bag at the back of the
room, then had to detour around the silent electric organ to
join the others up front. With linked hands, they walked down
the aisle together. She looked for sadness in the silent organ,
the empty benches, the strangers at the altar, the stormy night.
Joy kept breaking through instead.

They paced their steps together and reached the end of their
a capella processional with grace. Their attendants stood on
either side and Dr. Miller beamed at them, Bible in hand.

"Bonnie and John," he said solemnly, "I would like for you to
meet Miss Stapleton and Mr. Chap."

The older people all wore rimless glasses with little nose
pieces cutting into the flesh. Miss Stapleton's glasses were
smudged. Mr. Chap's coat didn't match his trousers. Bonnie
wished she could remember where she had seen him before.

Dr. Miller cleared his throat. "Shall we begin?"

The silence of the house of God fell around them, and they
straightened their shoulders and fixed their eyes on His

minister. Bonnie moved her hand so one finger touched a fingertip that pressed back.

"Dearly beloved, we are gathered together—"

Tears moistened Bonnie's eyes and she looked toward the floor. Dr. Miller's black shoes had stayed shiny through the rain. Her own black shoes pointed back toward his—*black!* Her sheer wool dress just cleared the tops of her old black boots. She gasped. John turned. The witnesses peered from the corners of their eyes. Dr. Miller finished his sentence and stopped.

"I'm sorry," she said. "I'll be right back. Sorry."

She hurried up an aisle that had no end. *Why didn't somebody tell me! I shouldn't be doing this. I remember, he's the church janitor.*

She changed to the white satin pumps while everybody inspected the floor and the furniture, then she started the long walk again. Mr. Chap came to meet her. He was taller than John, too thin for his clothes, with hair that was dark and straight, combed back and oiled, the ends rebellious. His face was a map of little lines, and his eyes behind the glasses were withdrawn, their expression sober. He bent his arm and extended it. Gently Bonnie laid her hand on his forearm, and they covered the remaining distance with dignity. He stepped back with a hint of a bow as he relinquished the bride, and moved to his former place.

"Dearly beloved, we are gathered together today to unite this man and this woman in holy matrimony."

Dr. Miller's voice was as rich and mellow as the paneled walls and warm as the candles. It supplied the missing music. The short ceremony gave her the sanctity and peace she had been seeking. The man she loved slid the narrow gold band onto her finger, and her hand held steady as it received the ring. Looking at the encircled finger, she thought of eternity. She felt relaxed, tired, married.

Mr. Chap did not speak or smile, but shook their hands firmly after the ceremony and backed away, quietly watching.

Miss Stapleton embraced Bonnie. She was graying, dowdy, resilient, and she smelled good. Close to Bonnie's ear she whispered, "How I envy you." To them both she said, "Bless you," several times.

Signatures were affixed to the marriage certificate, and less than half an hour after they had come into the church, they were leaving. They thanked everyone again. Bonnie broke away and went back to put her arms around Mr. Chap. When she kissed him on the cheek, she learned a secret. His cheeks were wet.

"My first wedding presents," she told John when they were alone. "Envy and tears."

When they were walking the four blocks to the hotel he asked, "What's that, envy and tears?"

"Miss Stapleton, she whispered that she envied me. I think that was sweet." *How can I explain? My friends weren't there.*

"I see. She cried for your mother."

"No, she didn't cry. Mr. Chap cried."

"He did? Son of a gun."

Sleet no longer assaulted them, but fog still lay against the buildings, absorbing the couple into its anonymous wetness.

He said, "You know, it *was* funny." On the word *funny* his voice broke and he put his hand over his face.

"You're laughing!" she wailed, hating him. "How could you?"

"I'm sorry." He walked away into the fog and she was alone.

He was back in an instant. "Oh, come on, Bonnie," he began again. "Can't you see this in the movies with the selected short subjects? You're too close to it; someday you'll look back and see."

"It was your wedding, too," she said. "Why aren't you too close to it?"

He took her hand. "They're good people who stayed late on a bad night for a couple of strangers. I am grateful, but can't you see? Ichabod Crane and Tugboat Annie, and the bride stopping the ceremony to change her shoes. What a script."

"It wasn't funny. It was my wedding, and it wasn't funny."

John sighed.

They walked on.

They passed the frosted windows of the Comanche Room. "How about a beer?"

She looked up. His eyes were teasing, flirting. Her stomach turned over. She rested her forehead against his shoulder.

They reached the lobby and approached the desk. As John talked to the clerk, Bonnie tugged at her gloves, exposing the left hand now ringed forever. She leaned her elbow on the desk, hand casually close to bell and blotter as he signed the register "Lieutenant and Mrs. John Blake."

Seven

The telephone bell pierced the dark. John moved after the second ring, breaking the seal of their bodies to throw off the covers. She adjusted the blanket carefully to preserve the warmth in his empty place as he sat on the edge of the bed.

The outline of his bare back projected from unfamiliar background shapes.

"Yes, thank you." The 11:00 call. He replaced the phone with a quick movement that added a muscular arm to the silhouette.

He dived back into bed after a brief skirmish with the rearranged covers that set them both giggling as they embraced again.

"Time to go," he whispered, while kissing the top of her ear.

"Thirty seconds more?"

"Oh, lady, you've got 'em."

It was several times thirty before he once again threw back the covers and found his way to the bathroom. The door closed and a ribbon of light appeared below.

Again Bonnie straightened the bed. The air chilled her arms and she pulled them under the blanket. Squirming and stretching, she savored the warmth and friction of sheets against her bare skin. She had discovered her body. The act of sharing it had brought personal discovery. The annihilation of the artificial wall had freed her womanness. How could she have been whole yesterday when she was more whole today?

Maxine had warned her the first time might be disappointing, even unpleasant. Maxine was wrong.

She had never before been so close to another human. Physically linked, locked together, for the first time in her life she was not alone. They exchanged the warmth of their flesh, mingled their body fluids. In his arms was a place—harbor, nest, cradle. She was in one act his mother and his child. Spiritually joined by their wedding vows, they would never be alone again. Yet she drew up her knees—already she felt severed.

"Where the hell did I leave my pants?" he swore under his breath as he stumbled across the unfamiliar room. The lamp came on. The florid little lamp base showed a colonial maid standing beside a pink and blue well. It sat on a dark desk-dresser next to a stack of hotel picture postcards, a Gideon Bible, and an almost full champagne bottle. Two water glasses still holding some of the stale spirits stood together at one side. White frost clouded the one small window.

John found his clothes piled on the luggage rack. He stepped into his officer's pinks and zipped up.

"We'll never be alone again," Bonnie said solemnly.

"You'd better be alone in about fifteen minutes or I'll be in the guardhouse. I'm not in a position to deal with M.P.'s tonight."

"Then you wouldn't have to leave tomorrow."

"I can't miss being on that plane." He relaxed his firm jaw and added softly, "I know what you mean, Bonnie. We'll keep remembering that."

He turned away and picked up his shirt. "I wish we could have had a nicer room." They hadn't remembered hotels were busy on weekends.

"It doesn't matter," she said, as she reached for the pale blue gown on the floor and pulled it over her head. "Are you sure you don't want me to go to the terminal?"

"We decided. It'd only be a few more minutes, sweet. This is a better place to say good-bye."

The words hung over them like smoke. She straightened her straps. *We should be saying important things.*

"Remember to see the guy I told you about. I think you can trust him to sell you a good used car. Lots of places take advantage of women."

"I'll remember."

"You'll have more money now. Try to loosen up a little."

"I'll try. John, are we rich?"

He stopped buttoning his shirt and frowned. "We talked about that. I told you I'm going to make my own way, although the annuity will help."

"But your parents. You keep mentioning servants and lodges—"

"Well, sure, Dad's pretty well heeled, but he's no Rockefeller." She didn't like the edge in his voice.

"I didn't mean—of course, I understand—well, it's just that I know so little about you." *He's wondering if I married him for his money.* "I mean what will it be like? Will I fit in?"

"You'll be my wife. Of course you'll fit in. In some ways you remind me of my mother."

"Oh, come on."

"You do. Short and pretty."

"All of that?"

He laughed and walked over to switch on the anemic overhead light. "Beautiful and well endowed." He leaned closer to the mirror to knot his tie. "Of course, I must admit you're going to be a bit of a shock to them tonight."

"Tonight?"

"Yeah, I'll get in line for the phone at the base. Mom and Dad are expecting the call about shipping out, but they aren't expecting a daughter."

This isn't happening.

"Will you call Sara?"

He kept working on his tie. At last he said, "I don't know, a letter would be easier. Yeah, I'll probably just write a letter."

"You know she'll hear it from your folks. It'll be hard on her."

"What is this concern? You want me to call her?"

"Not really, but I guess I can afford to be sorry for her."

"She wouldn't appreciate your sympathy."

He resents it, too. "Are you sure you never talked about marriage?"

"Not since we were twelve."

He isn't going to call her and I'm glad, but I shouldn't be. Poor girl.

She swung her feet out on the floor and hurried into the bathroom. She took care of her needs as quickly as possible, including a quick combing of the long hair, and buttoning into the lace-trimmed peignoir.

When she came out on bare feet, she stopped at the door. John stood at the window not moving, a shoe held in one hand. His shoulders were rounded, his head bent. She took a step toward him and stopped. *What is he thinking? I daren't ask.* She reached back and pulled the door shut with a click.

John straightened and looked hard out the window. He didn't say anything for a long half-minute, then smiled and said, "I do believe it's clearing. Maybe we won't be grounded after all." He sat down in the shabby chair and loosened the shoe laces.

She walked to the other chair and stroked the stiff military jacket that was draped around its back. She took it off the chair, holding it until he was ready. As she leaned her cheek against the collar, he accepted the caress with his eyes. He found the sleeves with his hands and she lifted the jacket high and wide over his shoulders. He buttoned the jacket, pulling it straight. After he picked up his cap by the visor, he laid his short coat across his arm. "Someday it will end and I'll watch you dress every day for the rest of our lives," he said.

She nodded. *Never. Never. This is the way it will always be.*

He held out his hands. She slid into her place. They tightened their hold and melted together, containing each other. He kissed her on the forehead and then on the lips. They pulled apart and he opened the door.

"Be careful," she said.

"You too."

Across the hall the elevator operator held the door. A soldier and a girl got on and turned around and watched. Three pairs of insolent, uncaring eyes blinked at them. He gave her a quick kiss, like a husband going to work, and hurried away. She shut the door before he could turn around, leaning heavily against it. *We never talked about dying.*

Slowly she moved back to the rigid armchair and lowered herself into it. Dry-eyed and wide-awake, she faced the dreary little room.

Lesson 1

Character

You have in mind persons you want to write about. You have met them in real life; you made them up; they are you; or (most probably) they were born from some combination of these origins. Write out a character sketch giving all kinds of details. List not only what characters look like, but their values, interests, education, occupation, fantasies, family background, etc. Be very selective about how many of these facts you pass on to your reader. A novel, of course, has room for more details than a short story. Don't use any more than necessary. But *you* must know, and everything your characters will do, the way they speak, they way they feel, is drawn from these details. Use their words in the dialogue, not yours. Use theme and plot to help the reader know them as well as you do.

The leading character in a story is called the protagonist. This is the character who is changed by what happens, who grows in some way. We're all changed a little by your story— the writer, the reader, the protagonist. The change may be small, subtle. The story usually also has an antagonist, who provides the tension, the other side of the conflict.

John is an antagonist for Bonnie because he is the catalyst propelling her into a different world, a different way of looking at life than she has experienced before. This function is as important to the plot as his romantic role. The result is delayed thirty years, but it finally happens, just from two brief meetings with John.

As characters are developed we say that they become more "rounded." There may be minor characters in the story who remain "flat" because they are not important enough to take up space for precise definition.

How many facts did you learn about Bonnie in Chapter One? The situation here makes it easy to supply the reader with facts about Bonnie's present situation and her past as she explains them to a new friend. It isn't always necessary to give so much information in the first chapter. The fact that much of the book is written from Bonnie's point of view is a big help in her character development. The reader is seeing everything through Bonnie's eyes, her perception, and this alone shows a lot about the kind of person she is.

You know early on that Bonnie and Maxine are young because I call them "girls." Young women in their early twenties were called "girls" in 1943. You also learn facts about Bonnie's character from things she does and says. She is a nice girl who avoids direct eye contact with the soldiers as she checks them out in the Comanche Room. She is compassionate, kind to the little sergeant as she rejects him, sorry for the waitress who will be left out of the party with the handsome lieutenant.

When John speaks of his involvement with the peace movement, Bonnie's reaction is, "He spoke of these things as though they were real, these things you read about, idealized, but didn't do." This is setting up her general attitude toward John and his unreal life that sticks with her after the marriage, and makes her unable to accept the possibility that there is a place for her in his "other world." After two years of correspondence and waiting, she will write to him in England asking for an annullment.

It was important to the development of theme and plot in my book to establish clearly Bonnie's character in the early part of the novel in order to show the gradual development of the woman she becomes by 1977, the end of the book. *Publisher's Weekly* said in their review of *Dear Stranger*, "The strength of this yarn is the way it looks at a woman changing over the years. . . ."

In 1943 she has clear-cut ideas about how a woman relates

to a man. At the bowling alley, "John was good; she was glad she didn't have to let him win." When John paces and thinks out loud about their getting married, Bonnie says, "'Well, when you make up your mind, let me know.'"

A scene in Part II mirrors a similar situation. It is 1977. Bonnie is divorced, she has been having an affair for some time with John who is still married. Once more he has been thinking aloud about finding a way that he and Bonnie could marry. This time she says,

"Wait a minute, John."

"She's always hated you. If she finds out about the past year. . ."

"John, wait a minute. Will you listen to me?"

"What?"

"I don't want to marry you, darling."

"What?" he said again.

"I said I don't want to marry you, love. I like the way we are."

This character has changed. Her wants are different, but more significantly, she knows what she wants now. Back then she waited for *him* to decide. The similarity to the scene in 1943 emphasizes the change.

The first impressions of John are of strength and *quality*. He occupies the center of attention at the table with his two friends when Bonnie first sees him. He makes her think of a doctor. Her first close up contact is:

As the waitress turned, a man's hand touched her drooping shoulders, a handsome gold watch showing from beneath a wool sleeve. Looking above wide shoulders, Bonnie contacted blue eyes that looked into hers and held. She recognized the dark-haired lieutenant she had been watching earlier.

Gold! Wool! *Quality*. Wide shoulders! When he speaks to the waitress she "straightened her apron and fluttered her hand across the crooked hair net." Observe the beginning of the development of a character who makes women tremble wherever he goes. When later at the table with the other lieutenants, the conversation seems to be slipping toward an off color tone, it's "'Drop it, Jackson,' John said, still looking at Bonnie." His casual (he didn't even look up) words are heeded, this is a man in control.

These are all happenings in the logical flow of the action, seemingly incidental, but they breathe life into the character. If you want to adjust the personality of a character as you rewrite, you can often do so with a few simple word changes. Suppose, instead of the above, I had written "John turned around in exasperation, 'Hey come on fellas, knock it off.'" Would this have given the reader a different picture of John?

When John first reappears in Part II (he is now fifty-five years old) Bonnie sees him seated at the banquet table. He is the scheduled speaker at the closing banquet of a large conference she has been attending in New York City.

He was a larger man than she remembered. Body thickened, hair a pleasant mix—grayer at the sideburns and above the forehead. She couldn't see his eyes, but she remembered the little half-smile he wore when his mind was somewhere else. He pulled back suddenly and the smile broadened as a waitress served his meal. The girl smiled, too, and backed into a waiter, bringing another serving.

The old boy hasn't lost it, he still sets waitresses' hearts aflutter! Again this is repetition of his introduction in Part I.

Minor characters who remain "flat" still show some individuality by very small touches. Note the church secretary who participates in Bonnie and John's wedding. She is mentioned briefly three times in the scene in the chapel (Pt. I, Chap. 6).

Two persons stood close to the altar. Bonnie recognized the fuzzy round figure of the church secretary.

The older people all wore rimless glasses with little nose pieces cutting into the flesh. Miss Stapleton's glasses were smudged.

Miss Stapleton embraced Bonnie. She was graying, dowdy, resilient, and she smelled good. Close to Bonnie's ear she whispered, "How I envy you." To them both she said, "Bless you," several times."

You do not know this character well, but she is not a blank. A few key words give you the impression of her that the point of view character receives by being there. You are there, too.

A later excerpt from *Dear Stranger*, the subway chapter, will show another example of the use of minor characters. Now I want to hear about your characters.

Assignment:

Outline in detail a character you would like to use as a protagonist in a fictional piece. This is not to be a story, just a list of
facts.

Example: Bonnie - Born 1922 in small town of Centerville in
midwest America. Graduated from Centerville Junior College
and moved to nearby larger city, Lancaster, about 1942, where
she worked as secretary to a minor executive in a defense plant.
She is petite, pretty, brown haired. Intelligent, naive, nice,
compassionate, loyal, thoughtful. Expects to find Prince Charming and get married and devote her life to a family. She has had
lots of boy friends, but lengths of relationships have been brief
because of the war. She will neck with a boy within limits, does
not even consider sex outside of marriage. She goes to church
every Sunday and sings in the choir. She is intelligent and has
intellectual leanings and capabilities she doesn't know she has
because the life and people around her do not bring them out.
    This is Bonnie, when *Dear Stranger* opens.

Comment: The above example may sound like a description
of a heroine in the familiar category of formula romance. The
difference is that formula romance heroines do not grow and
change. Rather, they are affirmed, just right the way they are.

Lesson 2

Theme

The theme is the statement made by the fiction. Never quote it in the body of your story, but know in your own mind what your story proves. Simply convince the reader as subtly as possible through the logic of the action. Crime doesn't pay. Crime does pay. You can't beat the system. Virtue triumphs. Good guys finish last. All politicians are crooks. A dog is man's best friend. Christmas is a lonely time. Families should stick together. Families stink. Remember: be subtle. Sometimes the theme may not be clear in your own mind until the story is well on the way, or even finished. You might make some discoveries about your own inner self when you read what you have said.

I have already mentioned that the theme of *Dear Stranger* is that it is never too late. A woman can continue to grow until she assumes control of her own life.

Some secondary themes are that love can last through the years; it's not a black and white world where right and wrong are clearly defined; sacrifice for the happiness of others is not always the best route for women (or the men in their lives); and that Prince Charming can exist, but his appeal to all women can cause problems. Did you notice any other themes?

Readers shouldn't be too aware of the theme in your story. They don't want to be manipulated by biased opinions. Slip it in as quietly as you can, as the consequence of a believable plot.

Escape fiction with its formula plots (some publishers of this type novels will furnish you with the formula upon request) does have a predictable theme, along with predictable everything else. Whether it is romance, western, mystery, sex and violence, they are all designed so that the reader will not have to think or feel deeply. They reinforce stereotypes and are not very close to real life. There is a place in literature for these, and some authors do very well writing them.

One mark of quality fiction is the extent to which it invites readers to think and feel. This treatise is designed to show you effective ways to do just that. A story that has this kind of depth and at the same time can be easily enjoyed as a "good read" is very marketable. It can reach multiple audiences at different levels.

Assignment I:

Think of some books you have read, or movies you have seen in which theme was of utmost importance. How was the plot manipulated to emphasize the theme?

Examples: Movie *And Justice For All* starring Al Pacino. The American system of justice is not equal for all citizens.

Movie *The China Syndrome* starring Jane Fonda, Jack Lemmon. Plants providing nuclear energy as a fuel are a threat America may not be able to control.

Movie *Star Wars*. Good always triumphs over evil.

Novel *1984* by George Orwell. The mechanization of society may lead to a dehumanized existence for humans.

Story *Christmas Carol* by Charles Dickens. Misers are lonely; generosity will bring happiness.

In these or in your examples, how was the plot manipulated to emphasize the theme?

Assignment II:

List some themes you might like to write about. Choose one that is appropriate for the character you outlined in the last chapter.

Assignment III:

Read the following excerpt from *Dear Stranger*, Part II, Chapter 9. This chapter was the ending of *The Woman I Am*. It is the climax, the turning point, of *Dear Stranger*. It is the moment of change, the beginning of new growth for Bonnie. All the secondary themes I mentioned are also brought to a climax in this chapter.

After Bonnie's marriage to John was annulled in 1945, she married her boss at the defense plant, Frank Forbes. In Part II, it is 1975, Bonnie is visiting her daughter, Anne, in New York City while attending an Earth Savers National Convention. She discovers that the speaker for the final Earth Savers banquet is John Blake, now an attorney of national prominence. After his speech, John leaves the hotel banquet room. After a few dances, Bonnie pleads a headache and leaves her friends to go to the hotel lobby.

Excerpt from *Dear Stranger*

Nine

When, in a small voice, she asked the desk clerk for Mr. Blake's room number, he smiled. "Yes, ma'am. I'll see if he's in." He picked up the house phone. "Whom shall I say—?"

"Mrs. Forbes." She fumbled in her purse, then snapped it shut. "I'm from the convention committee," she said in a raised voice to cover the lie. "I'm sorry to bother him so late, but there are some details we missed. It won't take long." Her voice trailed off. She was sure she was blushing.

The clerk didn't care. He talked to someone who answered, then told her, "Room 618. Go right up, Mrs. Forbes."

The self-service elevator stopped at six without a sound and the door slid open. The hall was modern and plush. The carpet red, the wallpaper silver-striped, the woodwork dark, the ashtrays streaks of unadorned chrome.

She thought of the halls at the Wheatland. In memory, probably wrong, they were narrow and badly lighted. Her mink became muskrat, her hair touched her shoulders. She tapped on the door marked 618.

They had exchanged places. The gently lamplit room was behind him when he pulled back the door, fastening the buttons on his jacket.

It wasn't the same. He looked older up close. She sensed a controlled annoyance behind the courteous smile.

"Hello. Mrs. Forbes? Come in."

He stepped back. Bonnie stayed.

Her rehearsed speech fled down the hall. "John," she said in a very weak voice. Then louder, "John, don't you know me?"

Slowly she watched the cool charm change to a puzzled, penetrating appraisal. The lines between his eyes deepened.

Like surfacing bubbles a joy emerged inside her. She felt
beautiful. *This is the way I always feel with John.* She laughed.

In slow motion he raised a hand and barely touched her
arm. "Bonnie? Is it Bonnie?"

She nodded. They were awkward, dumb. She laughed again.
His hand closed on her arm and he pulled her inside and shut
the door.

"I can't believe it."

They were standing very close, very still. It only felt like
each started and drew back at different instants. They were
familiar persons in different bodies.

"Well," he said, taking hold of both her hands. "Let me look
at you."

"You didn't recognize me."

"Well, of course you've changed. Who'd want to stay twenty-
one forever?"

"Yes, twenty-one. I was, wasn't I?"

He inspected her carefully and nodded. His eyes had turned
warm and happy. "Yes. Yes, it's good. You look just like you
should. I couldn't have planned it better."

She believed him. "I was very proud of *you* tonight."

"You were there? At the banquet?"

"Yes."

He moved behind her and took her jacket. She stood still
while he hung it in the closet.

"Are you really on the committee?"

They were in the parlor of a suite, a room of black leather,
chrome and glass.

"No. That was a lie."

There was a spring in his step as he came back and touched
her elbow. "Sit down. I was going to order a sandwich. I can't
eat when I'm speaking. What can I get you?"

"Maybe some coffee." She hadn't eaten much either, but the
thought of food made her sick.

"Some wine?" He smiled. "I remember you didn't like to
drink much."

She nodded, remembering the two highballs. "All right. I have learned to live with cocktail parties."

He waved toward the black chairs. She sat and placed her elbows on the glistening chair arms, turning her head to watch him at the phone. His fingers rested along the smooth, white plastic—long, large-knuckled, fingernails immaculate. A plain gold band encircled the third finger. *He has already touched me three—five—times, more than I can count.*

He came over and sat across from her. He spoke carefully, in a low confidential tone. "Well, girl, it's been a long time."

She shook her head. "Oh, yes."

His eyes sparked. "Jet planes and astronauts."

"Automatic washers and television."

"Beatles and —" he groped for a word.

"Beatnicks," came out in a rush of laughter. She kept wanting to laugh.

"That's not what we want to talk about. What about you? What's happened to you?"

She breathed out. "Did you marry Sara?"

"Yes. We've a silver anniversary coming up soon."

"Really? I—I thought it would have been longer."

"No. 1950."

I had my third baby that year.

"She had a brief modeling career. I knocked about a bit after I got my law degree. Worked a couple of places."

"I'm sure she's still beautiful."

Was there a slight hesitation before he said, "Yes, of course. Put on a little weight."

Bonnie tried to picture a fat Sara and failed.

"Forbes," he said. "Wasn't that the man you worked for?"

"Yes—Frank."

They weren't looking at each other now. His hand slid inside his coat and pulled out a thin cigarette case. After extracting a cigarette he started to close it, then remembered to extend the case to Bonnie. She reached across and took one. He lighted her cigarette and his before speaking again.

"Sorry, I don't think of you as a smoker."

"I started when the children were small. Now I'm trying to quit."

"Nasty habit."

She examined the toe of her satin pump.

"You have a family?" he asked.

"Yes," she responded quickly. "I—we have three daughters and two grandchildren. Linda and Karen are married, still in Lancaster. My youngest, Anne, is launching a career as a graphic designer here in New York. I'm staying with her now."

"Nice for you. They must be lovely young women, like their mother."

"Do you have children?"

"We had a son. He's dead."

"Oh, I'm sorry." She was. His pain showed.

"You accept it," he said slowly, "because you have to."

She waited for more, but he did not continue.

"Your parents—and Marc?" she asked at last.

"Dad died in 1954. Mother took over the business. She's still chairman of the board, going strong at seventy-five. Marc's president, but he's not really in charge. You probably didn't see it in mother, but there's a steel spine beneath that flowered chiffon."

I saw it! Poor Marc.

"Marc was such a sweet boy. I hope he's happy."

John hesitated. "I don't honestly think he is—very happy. He's one of those people who keeps missing the boat."

"Oh, John, why?"

"I suppose I shouldn't say that. Just because he hasn't followed the conventional pattern of marriage and working his way to the top."

"He's not married?"

"No. Know what he told me one time?"

"What?"

"That he hadn't been able to find a girl like Bonnie. That's what he said. You were his ideal."

Bonnie blushed. "Oh, my goodness. He hardly knew me."

John grinned. "You won people over rather quickly, remember?"

Her face grew warmer still. *How sweet it is.*

She looked down at her hands and said quickly, "My parents are both still in good health." *I'm acting twenty-one.*

John didn't respond and she looked up. "But that's right, you never met them."

"Your mother wrote to me several times," John said. "Nice, warm letters. I appreciated it. What about your friend—Laverne?"

"You mean Maxine."

"Yeah, I knew it was one of the Andrews Sisters."

They laughed suddenly and Bonnie had trouble answering. "Maxine just got her third divorce." The laughter didn't fit. She tried to stop.

He was laughing too. "That's too bad. Third one, you say."

They looked away from each other to gain control. She slowly stole a look at him, and they were off again.

A tapping intruded. John crushed his cigarette and went to the door. The waiter wheeled in a cart-table. As the waiter removed the two silver covers, Bonnie and John snickered. The waiter looked up, startled, then finished his task. With an injured air he accepted the tip and departed.

John shook his head. "Guy thinks we're off our rockers."

The funny business ended as quickly as it had started and they settled down on either side of the cart.

The covers had protected a dark sandwich and a plate of potato salad. The cart also held a chrome coffee carafe, a bottle of red wine, two white cups and two slender wine goblets.

"I can't eat alone."

"Well, maybe a little potato salad."

They looked at the single setting. John handed Bonnie the fork and picked up the spoon. "You start on that side," he said.

They looked at each other, not at the food. The cold silver handles balanced loosely. Slowly they lowered their eyes and slid tines and bowl under the tender, moist morsels. In ritualistic unison they raised the food from a common plate to their parted lips. Bonnie chewed and swallowed with difficulty. The fork awkwardly extended in midair, eyes focused on mayonnaise and pickle, she said, "John, why didn't you answer my letter?"

Carefully she placed the fork on the table and raised her eyes to his. The indentations over the bridge of his nose had deepened again. He spoke carefully.

"That's all done. We can't go back."

"I wish you'd try., I've carried questions in my heart for so long."

He said, "We had a trim, silver ship, propellers turning, engines roaring—and ceiling zero. They didn't let us get her off the ground."

Bonnie worked on the lump in her throat. "You must have been relieved when I ended it."

"I'm not a very humble person. 'Dear John' letters were bitter medicine."

"But you *were* relieved."

He sat back in the chair, his shoulders straightening in the trimly tailored tuxedo jacket. "I don't like post mortems. I think we should stick to the recent history of our relatives and friends."

"Maybe you'd like to discuss the current political scene."

"Ecology. We really took the big boys down in that court case, didn't we? It cost us money to defend the little guy, but we got a million dollars worth of publicity."

"Now you sound like Frank."

"Is that bad?"

"In this context it is. Relating everything to money."

"I don't do that. I'm sorry if it sounded that way."

"Would you have taken the case, just on principle?"

"I did. My partners hollered like hell, but I'm the senior partner. The old man backed me up."

"Sara's father?"

"Yes. He's in his eighties now, and his memory slips sometimes. We keep his name on the door, even though he doesn't do much. He was a brilliant man. I owe him a lot. I think I'll have a try at that sandwich. I'm starved. Sure you won't share?"

She shook her head. *How can he eat!*

"Finished with the potatoes?"

She nodded.

He poured two cups of coffee, set one on her side, and pulled the potato salad and sandwich plate closer. "So Maxine didn't hit it lucky in the marriage game?"

"No. She's still looking for Mr. Right."

"Well, I hope she finds him."

Bonnie silently watched John bite into the sandwich. She felt as though her wrists had been slapped.

"I suppose I should be going."

He put down the sandwich. "Oh, Bonnie, please don't. I've upset you. We're a couple of friends talking about old times. I don't look back much. What's done is done. A lot of things didn't turn out the way I wanted them to, but there's always something new around the corner. Or just the possibility of something new around the corner. Know what I mean?"

"You're saying there's still a future."

"Of course there is. Probably when I'm eighty, I can help some young guy of fifty-three change the world a bit."

"By then you'll have the answers."

"Oh, no. It's the young who know all the answers. The more alternatives you discover through the years, the harder it is to be certain of anything. The sweet ambivalence of choices! This can be the excitement that makes a day worth facing, or it can be scary as hell. Depends upon whether you decide to live excited or scared."

"Most of the people I know just live bored. They don't see alternatives."

"There's something to be said for that, too. There's security in black and white. Those of us wandering in the grays have our own kinds of problems."

"You'll always be my brave soldier."

"Oh, Bonnie, if you only knew. That's one thing about not getting airborne. We've kept our illusions."

"When weren't you brave?"

"How about this brave guy sitting on a bench in a railroad station for four hours, waiting for a train to get away from a town full of ghosts?"

"You? What town?"

"Lancaster. Christmas week 19—? 1946 it was. My first semester in law school.

"I spent Christmas break with a friend in Chicago. Decided on the spur of the moment to take the train to Lancaster. I didn't even know it was an eight-hour ride."

"Did you look for me?"

"Bonnie darling, why else would I go to Lancaster? I didn't know what had become of you. I didn't know anyone else there."

"You couldn't find me?"

"I found you. That's where the cowardice comes in. I went to your old address and your landlady told me. I couldn't face visiting you in a cottage. Chatting with your husband and bouncing your baby on my knee. She said you had a baby."

Bonnie remembered her world of diapers and dishpans. *That was the year we had the scrawny tree. Frank fixed the lights.* Tried to imagine John dropping into it. Wondered if it would have made any difference.

"You knew I married Frank."

"Yes, I did, but I'll have to confess I didn't recognize the name tonight."

She excused him, at the same time realizing that she could never hear the name "Sara" without remembering.

"Why didn't you answer my letter?"

"You don't give up, do you? What would any brave soldier do? Throw out your pictures. Throw a party. Throw up."

"I can't believe how you're evading me. You can't answer." She swallowed the lump and felt it slowly rise again. "I can take it. I just want to know."

"All right." He set down the coffee cup. "Because it damned near killed me."

Her defenses were set the wrong way. The blow came from behind. It wasn't fair.

She stammered, "I thought you wanted it. I thought I'd pushed you. That when you'd just needed a woman, I'd made you take a wife."

"You didn't say that. You said I was hurting you. You said there was another man."

"I thought you'd fight if you cared."

"I thought you'd write again and take it all back."

She stood up and walked to the window, turning her back. ANGELO'S the red neon sign said, ITALIAN CUISINE. She heard the muffled, unbalanced roar of traffic from below.

His soft voice reached her. "I wrote. Every day for a week."

She knew about tight crumpled wads of words scattered over the floor.

"Then I got legal papers. I signed them. 'Thanks for the memories' and 'Good luck'—I just couldn't say it."

She jumped when he touched her arm. The thick white carpet swallowed footsteps, and her nerves were surfaced and open. He slid both arms around her waist and put his face in her hair. She slid around, touching all the way, and reached her arms up around his shoulders. Drowning, drowning in the merging of mouths and tongues, clutching at the tuxedo jacket. She had never kissed like this before. The movement slowed and sweetened. She could feel his body changing. His hand moved across the front of her dress. Finding the little amber buttons. Releasing them, one by one.

A bell rang.

At the next shrill shout they stopped.

Reality grabbed her throat. The telephone was close by.

It rang again. She put her hand back on his arm and the sound struck again.

She jerked away and in a few steps picked up the phone. She held it out uncertainly. A loud voice came clearly from the receiver. "John? John, darling, are you there?"

John took two long strides to the back of the table and yanked at the cord. The plug flew out of the phone jack. Bonnie laid the dead thing on the table.

"I'm sorry," she said, looking at the floor. "I never could stand to let it ring." She added in a monotone. "That was your wife."

John moved slowly into the circle of light by the chairs and pulled the cart back. "No," he said flatly. "That was not my wife."

The leather chair back was soft and yielding, but she tried to steady herself against it. She was breathless and dizzy.

"You'd better sit down," John said. He uncorked the wine bottle and poured the red liquid into the stemmed glasses.

She edged around the chair and slid into it. She took the glass and lowered it to her knee as John sank into the chair opposite. Looking at the glass, the open bodice of her dress came into peripheral view, exposing cleavage and flesh-colored lace. The wine sloshed to the rim as she set the glass on the table. Her fingers rewound button loops around buttons, fingers lingering briefly across her bosom before locking together on her lap.

He watched without comment.

The wine soothed her tongue and warmed her throat. She watched the circles of light from the table lamps make overlapping shadows on the thick, white carpet into varied shades of gray.

Odd to sit, willing the pulse to return to normal, the blood pressure to go down. Odd to find the old feeling still there, like yesterday. Immaterial when yesterday was. The hungers,

*the primeval urge, not hidden as it had been before. This
time I know the beast. Friend or foe, it no longer lurks in the
shadows.*

They sometimes looked at each other, sometimes not.
They could still share an empathetic silence. Sorting out.

*You're not as cool as you look. Your pulse and blood
pressure need calming too. You want me again, but today the
beast has a new set of chains.*

He sat effortlessly straight, the very cut and cloth of his
clothes calling to something sweet and wild in her. She
looked at the hand resting on the chair arm and burned with
the feel of it slipping across the front of her dress. *How
would our child have been! A child from such sweetness. A
boy like his father, to cherish, to nurse at my breast, to love.*

"You'd have liked my boy." Her heart jumped. "Sara and I
had him. It's one great thing we did together. He was blown
to pieces by a land mine. We never saw him dead."

The grief from all the wars, all the dying boys she hadn't
mourned, came at once. "Viet Nam."

"Yes."

She waited for the next words, then groped for a question,
sensing his need to talk about it. "What—?"

"Different from our war. Did you think so?"

"Oh yes, I did. We had a protester, but she was a girl. She
didn't have to—"

"Brad was a protester. I helped him go to Canada. Gave him
money."

"Then—?"

"That's why it was such a waste. He was the type that
could understand dying for a cause, but it wasn't his cause."

Bonnie waited. He didn't need her questions.

"He was a bright boy—very bright. Graduated from Harvard at twenty. Such a day. Do you remember certain days
when you were really happy? It never came to us again, never
will. Just before we left, he let us have it. He wasn't staying in
school like we'd planned. Was leaving for Canada with his

friends. Sara had hysterics. She still showed her feelings then."

Bonnie nodded. She could see.

"We knew how he was about the war. Still, it was a shock. Your son, you know, you want him to be strong and brave. He had a low number. Once out of school it was the Army, Canada or jail. He thought staying in school would be the real cop-out. What do you think? What would you have done?"

"I guess it was his decision. You could only—"

"That's what I kept saying. And I had this growing feeling that he was right. Not like our war." He picked up the champagne goblet and twirled the stem between his fingers.

"He came back?"

"Yes. His mother got sick. He came back for her."

"Sara's sick?"

"It was emotional. She was hospitalized for a while. Withdrawn. She had a rough time. She couldn't help it. Her life was built around Brad and me. When we let her down she fell apart. She thought I was helping Brad to shame her."

"But you were doing it for yourselves, not against her."

He set the glass down hard. "I didn't even do that right. I didn't speak out after I knew the war was evil, that my country was wrong. It was more convenient to let my son take the rap. My clients, my associates, they wouldn't have liked my marching in parades or writing a book. I sent Brad money, but I'm not sure he knew I believed in what he was doing. I think maybe I told him, but I should have said it louder. I should have told him to stay."

"He was man. You couldn't have told him what to do, any more than anyone could have told you."

He looked at her sharply. "Do you really think so?"

"He had to know about his mother. He had to decide for himself."

He leaned his head on his hand, touching his forehead and looking at the floor. "He came back in time for his draft call. They got him. He was only overseas a month."

The ambiguous "they." The Army! The Viet Cong! His mother! His father!

"How is she?"

"She was okay after he went to the Army. Put on a bright face as though those months had never happened. When he was killed, she went through the expected motions of a grieving mother. If there's some terrible rage bottled up inside her, nobody saw it. Nobody got that close. Certainly not me. Yet, I could feel her holding on. I had this egotistical conviction that if I weren't there she'd break in two."

Tears were on her cheeks without her having cried them.

"And what about you? We all let you down."

Slowly his eyes focused on her. "Oh, Bonnie, no."

"I've never stopped blaming myself. I did it all wrong."

"No, you mustn't. I didn't want to make you feel bad."

"Why not? When you were alone, in a strange place and offering your life, I was the one who quit."

"Bonnie, listen to me. I wasn't always alone."

"What?"

"It was an unreal world—like a series of separate lives stretching from one mission to the next. Sometimes I took what comfort was offered. Do you understand?"

She shook her head slowly. The past couldn't change after it had been molded and fired and glazed and worshipped on an altar for half a lifetime.

"What do you mean?"

"How else can I say it?"

"You mean there were other women?"

He nodded. "Sometimes."

She felt detached, like a spectator at a play. "It never even occurred to me that you might be unfaithful. I never thought of it ever. Not once."

He shifted in the chair. Lifted his hands. "I'm an ass to bring it up. I just can't see you taking all the guilt."

Her eyes felt tight and hot. She labored with the words.

"What were they like? A different one every night? One that was special—?"

"No, no. Nothing like that." He leaned forward. "God, Bonnie, don't do this to yourself. It wasn't important. I can hardly remember. Something of the moment, 'a celebration—tonight I'm still here.' It had nothing to do with you."

"Was that what I was? Something of the moment?"

"You were the center of all my dreams of a sane, normal life."

"Why didn't you tell me?"

"I did, you know I did."

"Not at the end."

"You always represented all the things I wanted to come back to."

"Not Sara?"

"Not Sara. Everybody else decided that for me. Even you."

"I wanted life to be good for you."

"Bonnie," he leaned toward her. "Don't you see that it was your sacrifices that did us in? Not my transgressions."

She pulled back. A different kind of heat spread over her. "We were programmed to sacrifice, Sara and I. Living for our men and our children. They told us that to look for happiness in anything else, the way they could, was to be less than a real woman."

"I know that." They were the "differents," reaching across the divide.

"And you," she said slowly, "you *man*, with all your choices, you get to pick up the check." She could see it now, the bitter justice of it. "It doesn't come free."

He said, "That's man and woman. Now where does it leave you and me?"

She looked at him soberly. "Frank and I live black and white. We don't cheat."

"Just don't forget, lady," John said in a voice as quiet as hers. "Good old Frank is the son of a bitch who stole my wife."

She stood up. "I want to leave," she said. "I don't know how I'll feel tomorrow, but now I need to get out of here."

Rustily John rose and brought her jacket from the closet. Bonnie had never been so tired.

He put the jacket around her shoulders.

"I'll go down and get you a cab."

"You don't need to."

"I'm going out too."

"Oh."

She sounded young. Of course she's young. They don't say "Shit" to him.

He switched off the lamps, leaving a small one faintly illuminating the abandoned setting. They went out and he checked the lock. They walked down the hall and waited for the elevator without looking at each other.

The walls of the elevator were close. She stole a sideways glance at the silent figure sharing her isolation. They had been a pair once more—for a few hours. The door slid noiselessly open and the other people were there again.

At the far end of the lobby a revolving door stayed in motion. They wound through chattering groups, together but not touching. They each stepped into a moving compartment of the door without contributing to its momentum.

The doorman gave them the first cab and she hurried into it before John could help her. She scooted back. He leaned in and took her hand. "Will I see you again?"

"I doubt it. We could keep in touch. Maybe at Christmas."

He nodded. "Sure. Shouldn't wait another thirty years."

He hesitated, his hand still loosely covering hers. "Sometime, dearest," he said, "try doing it for Bonnie. The world will keep on turning."

A dull ache passed down her shoulder and into the passive hand. His fingers went away and he shut the door.

Her cab squeezed into the line of traffic, waiting for the light. In front of them, another taxi waited for a noisy group threading through the cars. Her driver swore under his breath as the delay caused him to miss the light. Bonnie saw John walk back to where the doorman watched for another cab.

She lifted her chin and pushed against the seat with her back. She was returning to the security of her cushioned box—static, stable. Only steps away, a New York sidewalk stretched toward an unknown horizon. The revolving door turned faster. Red lights flashed and faded on the backs of cars, on street corners, on moving neon signs.

Another cab pulled up and she watched John step toward it. He stopped, waited, waved it away with one quick motion. His head was bowed, his shoulders curved. She saw a young man in uniform before a frosted window, with a shoe in his hand and the same curve to his back. A private moment of resignation, fear, defeat, all things strong men deny themselves. *He's not Superman. He's a person like me. It's a celebration. Tonight we're still here.*

Her cab rolled forward. She frantically dug in her purse and pulled out a bill without looking at it. "Wait!" she called. "I changed my mind." She pushed the bill into the fare box and got out of the cab.

A noisy crowd was coming out of the hotel, moving against the people going in. The two groups collided and mingled and she was caught in the crosscurrent.

She raised her bent arms and with all the power she could muster plunged elbows into flesh and bone blocking her way. She heard gasps and unfriendly words—but the way opened.

She reached around the last human obstacle to close fingers around John's arm, feeling the muscle beneath the hard cloth. He straightened and turned his head. She held on, moving closer, their eyes pressing intimacies that had never been said. Silently she moved her hand down to lace her fingers into his, and, against the crowd, they walked together back to the revolving door.

Lesson 3

Plot

The third element is plot. The essence of plot is conflict. Without conflict, your story can't have much plot. Conflict and tension keep your readers on their toes—reading further. Conflicts are of two types: external and internal.

External conflicts come from outside the control of the protagonist (person experiencing the conflict). The Indians are attacking, the hurricane is approaching, the police are uncovering the crime. External conflicts are resolved by action.

The development of the early romance of Bonnie and John is in external conflict with World War II and John's military obligations. The action they choose to take is an ill-advised marriage.

Internal conflict goes on inside a character. Internal conflicts are resolved by decisions, choices. *Show both sides*, let the reader share the dilemma. If the choice is one-sided, easy to make, the plot will not be engrossing.

If she loves two men, that's internal conflict. If one of their wives is coming to call, that's external.

Dear Stranger has more internal conflict than external. Decisions must often be made about: marriage? sex before marriage? give John back to Sara and his interrupted life in Boston? end her own limbo state in a marriage which may be doomed anyway?. In Part II, commit adultry in the celebration of a rare second chance? end a marriage of thirty years? decline help to a daughter who needs a chance for a career? become a man's regular mistress? and many more.

Quality literature uses more internal conflict. Commercial or escape fiction uses more external. Stories written expressly for a male audience, as in men's magazines, tend to rely on external conflict (action) more than stories directed to a female audience (feelings). Many excellent stories, of course, contain both in varying degrees.

Build the major story conflict to a climax or turning point (where the action reverses) at about the middle, then wind down, leading to a resolution at the end. Don't be soft hearted, do everything you can to make the conflict a gruelling one. Readers like to suffer; the triumph or capitulation at the end will be intensified.

Resolution of the conflict should be brought about by the protagonist, unless you have a specific reason for showing the character's inadequacy, or impotence. The protagonist usually has the crooks tied up before the police arrive.

Tension can be hard to live with in real life, but in a story it holds the readers' interest, keeps them turning the pages. Tension is created in small ways throughout the story. It can be present in a very inactive scene such as in a conversation between two characters. They may be antagonistic toward each other, or just uncertain about where they stand— sometimes pleasantly so. The tension doesn't have to be a bad thing. Probably no other kind of tension is used as much in literature as the natural tension that exists between men and women. This is something that is universally understood—the perpetual game playing that goes on between people of the opposite sex.

Notice how the tension is indicated at the point of Bonnie and John's first meeting in the Comanche Room.

"Excuse me." His voice was pleasant and low, a clipped accent separating the words. "Before you order, how about considering the case of three lonely soldiers. It's two long hours till curfew." He turned back to the waitress and smiled as he asked, "Can you take the order at our table—that is, if these ladies will join us?"

The waitress straightened her apron and fluttered her hand across the crooked hair net. He turned back to Maxine and then to Bonnie. "I'm John," he said.

Bonnie heard a distant voice saying, "I'm Maxine." *If we had gone straight home tonight this wouldn't be happening. He has been watching me. He saw me reject the sergeant.* She said, "I'm sorry; we really should be going."

Maxine frowned and squirmed.

Placing both hands on the table edge, John leaned down. She strained to catch his words. "Please come. Just for a beer. We won't even ask your last names. A month from now you won't remember, but we will."

I'll remember. I'll remember. "We really shouldn't, but—"

John straightened up and reached for Bonnie's coat.

"That's not my table," the waitress said. She looked tired again.

"Thank you, you've been very helpful," Bonnie said. She felt a ridiculous impulse to embrace the girl.

John folded her coat across his arm. The fur clung to the wool uniform, filling in the spaces between his arm and body. Bonnie slid from the booth into the aisle. Their eyes met and turned away.

Maxine pulled her coat about her shoulders and, chatting comfortably, picked up her hat. Bonnie heard not a word.

Bonnie's consistently saying something different than she is thinking; her nervous impulse to embrace the waitress; Bonnie's and John's eyes meeting and turning away; these things are all part of the action and dialogue, moving the plot, but they also pass along to the reader a feeling of tension. This scene came from the point of view of a romantic young girl, so it is a romantic young scene.

The Woman I Am ended where Bonnie turned around and went back into the hotel with John in New York City on the night they found each other after a thirty year separation. This is probably the most exciting resolution of a conflict in the book, and it made an impressive ending for my first short published work. It did, however, seem to me and to many of my readers to be even more of a turning point, and we all needed to know what happened next. The only way I could find out was to keep writing, and that's why I wrote a sequel. The sequel by itself was not complete, as it was only the last half of the story. I needed both sides of that moment when she got out of the taxi, and I made a successful decision when I regained the rights to *The Woman I Am* from Dell and combined the two books. The hotel scene then became the turning point in the middle of the book.

Tension is created for readers by building suspense, hinting at things to come, withholding information. Be sure though that you have told them enough, made them care enough, involved them enough, to make them want to find out the rest. Surely the suspense value of the scene where the young lovers meet again, after a thirty year total separation, is very great. All that has gone before has built toward that moment. The lovers feel young again, relive the tension, but the point of view character is now a fifty-three year old woman. She knows and says what she thinks (I didn't need to use the italics very often to show Bonnie's contradictory thoughts in the sequel), and she no longer has romantic expectations from life. This is the high point of the story, appropriately appearing now in the middle of the book where the climax is supposed to be. I rewrote the scene over and over again, discarding one final copy after another. The way they spoke, the way they related, every word they said, established something about their character; and at this important moment, it had to be just right.

For example, earlier versions had John bursting out early in their conversation with an emotional admission that he had been badly hurt when he received Bonnie's Dear John letter. When I was bothered by the turn things had taken I realized that a "real man" would not be so anxious to speak of his feelings, that he would be inclined to avoid such an admittance. In the final version, he only speaks of this much later after Bonnie has asked him repeatedly.

There also was a point at which things seemed to be dangerously approaching a Little Red Riding Hood and the Big

Bad Wolf image of the two. Of course this wouldn't do at all. Bonnie is a big girl now, and in no way do I want the readers to think she is being innocently led astray.

The hours I spent rewriting this scene paid off, I feel that the final version successfully finishes the first part of the story, and sets the stage for the next part. This chapter required no alterations when *The Woman I Am* was incorporated into *Dear Stranger*. The action that Bonnie took on the last page of that chapter when she turned her life around by stopping the cab and returning to the hotel was a logical sequence, one that I would expect most readers to be rooting for.

A plot must be believable. Your knowing that it really happened is not enough if it doesn't sound credible. If the situation is a fantastic one, as in science fiction, the characters must still react to it in a believable fashion.

A plot that is well outlined in advance can make your writing easier, with at least the climax (turning point) and resolution already thought out. However, sometimes a writer starts working on a story without knowing for sure how the conflict will be resolved. As the character and situation take on life, the way out reveals itself. You will have to decide if you want to take this chance.

Example: Following is a short plot outline of *Dear Stranger*:

> 1943 Bonnie & John meet and marry
>
> 1944 Bonnie visits John's family in Boston, meets Sara
>
> 1944-45 Bonnie gets to know her boss, Frank Forbes
>
> 1945 Bonnie asks for an annullment, marries Frank
>
> 1975 Bonnie attends Convention in New York

Flashbacks fill in intervening years

After John's speech at convention, Bonnie visits him in his hotel room

TURNING POINT: For the first time in her life, Bonnie makes a decision on her own to take what she wants. She spends the night with John.

> 1975 Bonnie returns home, sees herself as only an appendage of members of her family. Decides to leave family to go to New York and "find herself"
>
> 1975-77 Takes part-time job, writes novel, goes to college
>
> Has sexual liason with John, plus one-nighters with two younger men she has known before and cares for
>
> Prepares for conference in Paris, and publication of her novel
>
> 1977 Open ending shows Prince Charming (John) yearning for her

Resolution: In spite of conflicts and challenges, Bonnie is in control of her life at last.

This outline was constructed after the fact. I began with some ideas about nostalgia for a certain time period, and a beginning and an end. Actually, the resolution is the same for both books; the descending action just amplifies the resolution suggested at the climax. *Dear Stranger* also contains some sub-plots and conflicts that aren't mentioned in this outline.

A detailed outline would be more essential for a different type of book. A mystery story, or one with many interlocking developments would need to be planned more carefully. But when your novel relies heavily on human emotion and interaction, it may be enhanced by giving your characters lots of freedom.

Assignment I:

1. Using a character you have outlined, describe a life situation that places him/her in conflict.

Example: In 1943, a young girl meets a lieutenant who is stationed at the air base in her town. They fall in love, but will only have a week together before he will be shipped overseas.

Assignment II:

Get more specific. For a short story, outline one segment of the problem, one specific, significant episode in which the character must deal with some aspect of the larger conflict and make some progress toward resolution, some growth or change. Where and when will the action take place? What other characters will be involved? If you are thinking in terms of a novel, this could be one important chapter of a longer story.

Remember it will always be okay to change your mind as you write. Don't be afraid to experiment, you need not be committed to any plan. This is one of the few places in life where you play God, in control of the universe. The exception might be when your characters take on a life of their own and run amuck with your careful plans for them.

Example: Bonnie and John have one last stolen evening together before he ships out. Their wedding planned for the next day has been cancelled, but they have a few hours. What will they do? What will they say? What lifetime decisions will they make? When I wrote this chapter I placed them in the situation, started the dialogue, and waited to see what would emerge. (Reread Part I, Chapter 5.)

Dear Stranger is filled with decision-making situations, large and small. Every conflict, even an unimportant one, pulls your readers on a little further. It's "I couldn't put it down" bait. This is especially true if the plot is not predictable.

Open *Dear Stranger* several places at random. What is going on? Is a situation developing that will entail a decision? Most chapters have their own conflict and resolution.

Lesson 4

A Short Story

A novel (roughly starting at 75,000 words) has multiple themes and conflicts, may have several story threads running through. Still, the structure is built around one overall theme and conflict. A novelette or novella is constructed more like a novel than like a short story. In length it falls between the two. "Book-length novels" in magazines are usually this length.

A good short story contains *nothing* that does not contribute to development of theme, character, or plot. A short story is more difficult to write than a novel because of this necessity for unity. The smaller canvas requires more precision.

Let your story find its own length. You might want to cut or add for other reasons, but don't do it just to fit a predecided number of pages. Your short story idea may turn into a novella (or vice versa).

A short story contains less than 10,000 words. Standard lengths for magazine stories are 1,500, 3,000, 5,000. Count words by multiplying the average number of words in a line by the average number of lines on a page. Lines that are not full (as in dialogue) are counted as though they were full. Don't let the short story cover too much material. A vignette recreating the mood of a small conflict in its total is better than a sketchy telling of a complicated plot. Save the complicated plot for your novel.

Some of the chapters in *Dear Stranger* could stand alone as short stories. The following, Part II Chapter 28, is one of these. It is the first chapter in *Dear Stranger* that departs from Bonnie's point of view, the first half being written from the point of view of her daughter, Anne. It could be understood without explanation about what has happened before, but since you are following the complete plot, I will tell you that Bonnie has left her husband and is living alone in New York City.

Excerpt from *Dear Stranger*

Twenty-eight

"Tell me when Santa Claus comes by." Anne Forbes opened the oven door a crack, just to enjoy the sight of the big Thanksgiving bird. A peek helped its aroma escape to creep into every corner of the efficiency kitchen and to wander on beyond.

She barely heard the "Hummmm?" that came from Bill, relaxed on the sofa with the *Times* obstructing his view. The television set in front of him was chronicling Macy's Christmas parade, taking place at that moment not far away. Bill in his old jeans and a T-shirt reading "I love New York" half-reclined, with his bare feet on the sofa.

"Santa," she said again. "I want to see what the old boy looks like this year."

"Why? He's not going to bring you anything. You're too old."

Anne took a wooden spoon from the rack and sent it spinning. It reached its target with a splat, pulling the *Times* from Bill's fingers and into his face. He swung his feet to the floor and hollered, "Hey!"

Anne stood grinning, hand on hip. "You're supposed to be running the sweeper, Smarty."

Bill settled back on the sofa. "Soon."

"Come on, Bill. Mother'll be here any time now."

"Why do we always have to run the sweeper before your mother comes?" Bill mumbled from behind the paper.

"It's Thanksgiving. The house is supposed to be clean on Thanksgiving."

Bill slowly lowered the paper. "Why?"

"It just is. Didn't you grow up with a clean house for Thanksgiving?"

Bill grimaced and cocked his head. He started to raise the paper, then lowered it again. "But my father didn't run the sweeper."

"Well, things have changed. You do."

Bill grinned and said "Okay." He raised the paper. "Soon."

Anne shook her head and took the sweet potatoes out of the refrigerator. At the sink, she peeled them.

She heard Bill say, "Does your mom know we're going skiing over Christmas?"

"No. She'll probably go home."

Linda's tearful voice on the phone came back to Anne. "Whatever will we do about Christmas?" Last May that was. When the sisters first faced together the black news that their parents were parting. "Oh, Linda," Anne had said. "There are more important things to worry about."

"But what will we do? Who do we spend it with? Who gets left out of dinner?"

"Well, if Mom is still in New York, she can eat with us."

"Still in New York?" Linda had quavered. "She won't stay there. She'll never do that."

"Well, wait and see," Anne had said, impatient with her oldest sister, who was the least self-reliant one. Yet, the time was getting close and Anne wondered what they were going to do about Mother.

"She should be here by now," Anne said to Bill. "Oh, God, I forgot to tell her about the parade!"

Bill put down the paper. "Anne, she's a grown woman. She'll find out about the parade. It's out there."

"But she was going to bring a pie. All those people!"

"You treat her like an infant. You do."

"Well, she didn't put an extra lock on her door. And she forgets things."

"She's made it fine for six months. Give her credit."

"Do you like her, Bill?"

"Yeah, sure. Of course I like her."

"We should have her over more often. I've neglected her."

Bill got up, came into the kitchen and put his arms around Anne. "Honey, your mother's tough."

Anne pulled back. "What do you mean by that?"

"I mean she doesn't need you to hold her hand. She has a boyfriend, doesn't she?"

"That's another thing. I think she does. And he's married."

"Well, so's she."

"That's not funny, Bill."

She turned around and picked up the paring knife. "How could anyone change so much? She always did what Dad wanted her to. And she was so—so—well, controlled."

"I think she's terrific. You've got to let go, Anne."

"I don't want her to get hurt."

"I told you, she's tough. You'll see."

At that moment Bonnie was spreading her feet, balancing in place as her purse arm curved around a slippery pole, the other holding a plastic-wrapped pumpkin pie. With olympic precision she maintained her balance as the subway car bounced and jarred, started and stopped. The car was packed. She had fought her way in, vying for standing room. The door closed swiftly and silently, sending some people jumping back on the platform. She held her ground by the vertical pole. There was no way she could reach the high bar and balance the pumpkin pie.

Persons seated along the side stared vacantly ahead, solemnly ignoring the closeness of the swaying crowd. A well-dressed elderly man held his head erect before the red graffiti scrawled across the new paint, his dignity belying the ugly word on the wall. The lady next to him obviously belonged with him, although they did not speak to each other. She wore the same kind of 1950s elegant air, clothing conservative and new. And the hat . . . stirring memories of the days when every woman on the street in Manhattan wore a hat. The young girl on his other side sat just as close, but her darkly outlined sad eyes and frosted pink lips placed her in a different milieu.

The car was so crowded. Pressure from behind grew more persistent. As she edged forward, the pressure followed. With growing horror, Bonnie identified the object pressing against her. The woman in the hat watched, jaw dropping.

Bonnie pivoted her head toward a dirt-streaked red nylon jacket. She forced her eyes up to the young face bearing a humorless smile and eyes without human softness. His cold steel eyes bore into hers, undressing and raping. His head slowly sank as his knees bent and his pelvis rotated against her hip.

Lights exploded and streaked, muscles jerked and rolled, and with the other passengers Bonnie watched her Thanksgiving dessert ooze and slide down stubbled cheeks. The crust in its foil pan covered his face briefly, then slid between them before careening to the floor as they wrenched apart. The plastic had protected his nose, forcing the spice-brown pumpkin out the sides into his hair, and off the edges of his chin onto the red jacket.

A murmur spread through the crowd like rising wind, expanding to laughter and cries of approval from persons close by, while others farther away craned their necks and asked each other what was happening. Bonnie felt the tone of the crowd sweep toward approval and she was suddenly onstage, in the spotlight, adored by the audience. Without a hearing, the man had been condemned. Bonnie did not dare look at him. She feared him, as she feared snakes and rodents. She feared the loathing that had moved her to violence.

Passengers held on as the car lurched to a stop. The block letters on the walls of the station said Times Square. Bonnie pushed her way to the door and escaped to the platform just before the door slammed shut. She looked back to see the train start up with the pie-faced man still aboard. Relief made her knees give way and she leaned against a post.

"Are you all right?" The kind voice came from the well-dressed man she had stood by on the train. He and the young girl with the sad eyes looked on with concern.

Bonnie nodded. "I guess so." She tried to relax her chattering teeth.

"I saw him," the girl hissed. "The son of a bitch had it coming."

Bonnie nodded again. Nausea and dizziness were receding. Strength returned to her noodle knees.

Smiles slowly emerged from the man and girl. "I shoulda had a camera," the man said. "You shoulda seen his face!"

The three of them roared together, suddenly close.

"Sure you're all right?" the man asked again.

"Yes, I'm sure," Bonnie answered, looking out at the name on the approaching train. "What a mob today."

"It's the parade."

"I know."

They turned away from each other and she stood alone again in the crowd, wondering where she could find a bakery doing business on Thanksgiving.

Several characters made cameo appearances here. Again, we only saw and knew about them what Bonnie saw and knew as the point of view character.

Bonnie pivoted her head toward a dirt-streaked red nylon jacket. She forced her eyes up to the young face bearing a humorless smile and eyes without human softness. His cold steel eyes bore into hers, undressing and raping. His head slowly sank as his knees bent and his pelvis rotated against her hip.

This man was definitely a one-dimensional character, totally evil, because that was the only side of him Bonnie ever saw.

I introduced three other characters into this brief scene, mostly to provide visual background, but they ultimately also contributed to the larger picture of Bonnie's experience as a midwesterner in the big city.

Persons seated along the side stared vacantly ahead, solemnly ignoring the closeness of the swaying crowd. A well-dressed elderly man held his head erect before the red graffiti scrawled across the new paint, his dignity belying the ugly word on the wall. The lady next to him obviously belonged with him, although they did not speak to each other. She wore the same kind of 1950s elegant air, clothing conservative and new. And the hat. . . .stirring memories of the days when every woman on the street in Manhattan wore a hat. The young girl on his other side sat just as close, but her darkly outlined sad eyes and frosted pink lips placed her in a different milieu.

This is Bonnie's original impression of them. It progresses and changes as the action proceeds. I didn't plan ahead for this, it just worked out as the characters wrote the story for me.

"Are you all right?" The kind voice came from the well-dressed man she had stood by on the train. He and the young girl with the sad eyes looked on with concern.

Bonnie nodded. "I guess so." She tried to relax her chattering teeth.

"I saw him," the girl hissed. "The son of a bitch had it coming." Bonnie nodded again. Nausea and dizziness were receding. Strength returned to her noodle knees.

Smiles slowly emerged from the man and girl. "I shoulda had a camera," the man said. "You shoulda seen his face!"

The three of them roared together, suddenly close.

"Sure you're all right?" the man asked again.

"Yes, I'm sure," Bonnie answered, looking out at the name on the approaching train. "What a mob today."

"It's the parade."

"I know."

They turned away from each other and she stood alone again in the crowd, wondering where she could find a bakery doing business on Thanksgiving.

In this brief sequence I have made the points that it is dangerous to make assumptions from people's looks (the man was not with the woman who looked like his mate); even in the big city people are often kind and concerned about each other; and brief contacts with other human beings can be significant, both good and bad.

The Thanksgiving chapter contains all the elements of a complete short story. The points mentioned in the above paragraph are all themes, although the main theme which develops from the beginning of the chapter is "Mother is tougher than her daughter gives her credit for."

If your characters, both major and minor, are real people, the things that happen to them, the contacts your point of view character has with them, will be felt by your readers. Run the risk of absorbing viewpoint characters into yourself the way an actor would. The first step is to become your point of view character. The step that follows is to find the words that will transmit this identification to your readers.

Assignment:

Write out an explanation of why this is a complete story. We have discussed theme and character development. Can you outline a plot? What was the turning point or climax? Who is the protagonist, how was the protagonist changed? Who is the antagonist, how did the antagonist cause the change? Does this story only include material that develops theme, plot, and character?

Lesson 5

Point of View

More than half of *Dear Stranger* is written in the limited omniscient point of view of the protagonist, Bonnie. There is no set way point of view must be handled, but the story will be more within your control if you understand your options and use them to establish the kind of communication with your reader that works best for your fiction. This can be a powerful tool. It is extremely important.

I will be throwing a lot of terms at you, which may be confusing at first, but point of view is possibly the most important part of fiction writing technique, and once you understand the terms their use will become automatic, believe me.

Whose eyes, whose mind is recording what the reader finds in this story? In most twentieth century fiction, the author remains invisible, creating a bridge between characters and readers.

Camera Eye

The most distanced viewpoint is the camera eye, telling only what could be seen by a camera (no inner thoughts). The first ten paragraphs of *Dear Stranger* are camera eye.

Example: These are the opening paragraphs of *Dear Stranger*:

1. *She was young in 1943—when the girls were red-lipped and virginal, and the measure of time was the duration.*

2. That Friday, the February wind hurtled around buildings and scooted across the dirty snow that had packed down and refrozen after dark. Bonnie and her best friend scurried into the protection of the heavy revolving door and pushed it, groaning and resisting, to deliver themselves into the warm confusion of the Wheatland Hotel's Comanche Room.

3. The wind had polished their skin pink and fringed their high hair-dos, but the little felt hats perched on the crowns of their heads still neatly divided pompadour from pageboy. Dribbles of brown water slid from their victory-rubber boots onto the dark tile floor as they surveyed the room. "See a place?"

4. Mixed voices rose and fell over the clink of silverware and glass—noise overlaid with smooth, sweet swing flowing from the jukebox, horn notes as neatly clipped and in place as a G.I. haircut.

5. The men of the U.S. Army Air Corps colored the room olive drab; the bright dots were hairbows and skirts and an occasional civilian necktie. Savory smells of hamburger and onions and fresh-baked apple pie drifted from booths. Up front a veil of smoke hovered over tables weighted with Schlitz and Pabst Blue Ribbon.

6. The girls spotted a couple leaving a booth, and hurried to claim the space.

7. The waitress stacked the dishes and pushed them to one side as with her other hand she wiped the dark, varnished tabletop, and with a last quick move, emptied the ashtray onto the saucer that topped the stack. "Be right with you," she called back as she walked toward the kitchen. The girls slid into the booth, facing each other.

8. Bonnie pulled her arms out of the muskrat coat and arranged it behind her, stuffing gloves into the pockets. "I filed all day. Mr. Forbes was out of town."

9. Laying back her coat, Maxine regarded her distorted reflection in the chrome napkin holder. "I noticed you weren't at your desk," she said as she unpinned her hat and smoothed her curly blond hair. "What about Alice Faye settling for Don Ameche? I'd have waited for Tyrone Power any day."

10. Bonnie shrugged. "Maxine, if only we had such a problem!"

11. As she spoke Bonnie looked around the room, carefully avoiding direct eye contact. Many of the men wore the dark green coats of army officers with one gold bar mounted on each shoulder and new silver wings pinned on their chests. From across the room they looked alike—youthful, lithe bodies, close-cropped hair, uniforms.

12. Three lieutenants sat together not far from the jukebox, and Bonnie found herself watching the flowing gestures of the dark-haired one in the center who was doing most of the talking. *Good hands. Maybe a doctor.* She tried to put him in a white coat, but it was hard. He looked so good in the uniform. His right hand suddenly became a fist and landed hard on the table. She jumped, then felt relieved when she saw them all laughing. She was glad he wasn't angry, and sorry to have missed the joke.

13. "Evening, girls."

14. A soldier leaned over their booth and gripped the table edge, swaying slightly until he found his balance. He was a small man, lean and wiry, with weathered, leathery skin like a farmer. He wore the stripes of a buck sergeant, and gunner wings.

Imagine this as a movie. You can see it all. In paragraph 7 which begins, "The waitress stacked the dishes...," the camera zooms in for a closeup. Mystery or suspense can be heightened by use of a camera viewpoint. But remember, the biggest advantage the printed page has over plays and movies is its option to show the characters' thoughts and feelings, so think carefully before you give this up.

Limited Omniscient

The mood is more intimate, the reader's involvement more personal and complete, when you use a limited omniscient viewpoint and stay at all times within one character's mind. This can be done in first person ("I" narrator) or in third person (he, she). In either first or third person limited, everything is as this person perceives it. The description is what she sees, dialogue is what she hears. In *Dear Stranger*, actual words of Bonnie's thoughts are given occasionally, in italics (more about this later). Nothing can be shown that this character doesn't know.

Dear Stranger is written in third person. We move into Bonnie's mind in Paragraph 11, with the phrase, "As she spoke Bonnie looked around the room..." She sees the three lieutenants, and wonders if one could have been a doctor. We couldn't know that she felt relieved to see them all laughing if we weren't in her point of view. It is Bonnie (not the author) who thinks the lieutenant looks like a doctor, and the sergeant like a farmer. She is a midwestern girl, you know. We will stay in her point of view until well into Part II of the book. It soon becomes unnecessary to say "she thought" or "it seemed to her" because the readers know (subliminally from the way the narrative flows when it has been written by an aware author, not because they ever heard of limited omniscient) that they are looking out of her eyes.

The story could be told in exactly the same way, still limited omniscient viewpoint, if all the third person pronouns (Bonnie, she, her, them, etc.) were changed to first person pronouns (me, I, us, etc.). The difference would be that all the narration would be coming from Bonnie, and the author would have to remember to use her vocabulary and speaking habits. Let's try this substitution beginning at Paragraph II where the point of view becomes limited omniscient.

As she [Maxine] spoke, I looked around the room, carefully avoiding direct eye contact. Many of the men wore the dark green coats of army officers with one gold bar mounted on each shoulder and new silver wings pinned on their chests. From across the room they looked alike—youthful, lithe bodies, close-cropped hair, uniforms.

Three lieutenants sat together not far from the jukebox, and I found myself watching the flowing gestures of the dark-haired one in the center who was doing most of the talking. Good hands. Maybe a doctor. I tried to put him in a white coat, but it was hard. He looked so good in the uniform. His right hand suddenly became a fist and landed hard on the table. I jumped, then felt relieved when I saw them all laughing. I was glad he wasn't angry, and sorry to have missed the joke.

You can see, this works pretty well, although the tone *could* be more informal in first person.

From across the room they looked alike—young and athletic, GI haircuts, uniforms. Three cute lieutenants were sitting together not far from the jukebox and I found myself watching the dark-haired guy in the center who was doing most of the talking.

But this substitution would not work at all in the opening paragraphs which we have identified as camera eye, because a limited omniscient narrator wouldn't describe *herself* in the same way that an outside eye would.

The wind had polished our skin pink and fringed our high hairdos, but the little felt hats perched on the crowns of our heads still neatly divided pompadour from pageboy.

The limited omniscient narrator wouldn't be as aware of her pink skin and fringed hairdo as an outside eye. Injecting naturally a physical description of the point of view character can be a problem. The most common device is to have him/her look in a mirror. You may think of other ingenious ways to do it.

Readers automatically identify with the point of view character, and this tends to make them more sympathetic to and understanding of this character. Haven't you found yourself rooting for the murderer's getaway when you have been inside his/her mind throughout the perpetration of the crime? This is one of the ways an author can manipulate through technique. The author puts the reader in the protagonist's shoes, creating instant empathy.

Another variation is to make the point of view character a minor one, not the protagonist. One well-known example of this is Dr. Watson in the Sherlock Holmes stories. In *Dear Stranger* I could have written from Maxine's viewpoint. An obvious handicap would have been she would not have been present when Bonnie and John were alone, could not have conveyed what happened there except by hearsay. In the Sherlock Holmes series, Doyle probably chose a companion of Holmes' as the point of view character in order to keep the mystery going. He didn't *want* the reader to know everything that Holmes did.

The "unreliable narrator" is an interesting point of view approach. The limited point of view character gives us all the facts as he/she sees them, but draws a different conclusion than we do. We figure out that things are not as they seem.

My principal male character, John Blake, is always seen through someone else's eyes until the final four pages of *Dear Stranger*. He retains a certain mystique in this way. What is he really like, inside? Bonnie doesn't know, but readers for a long time only see him through her eyes—Prince Charming who can do no wrong, doorway to a different world. Eventually, he appears in a different setting through his brother's eyes—as envied older brother, favored son, Sara's unfaithful husband. And finally, as a long withheld treat, readers at last get inside his head.

Omniscient

Within *un*limited omniscient, the author assumes the powers of the almighty, seeing all, knowing all. This is what that big word really means. It also allows the reader access to the inside of people's minds, but it differs from *limited* omniscient in that it sees inside everyone, and is not limited to one character. Jumping from one head to another in each paragraph can be confusing to readers, not allowing them to identify. This is a weakness often found in the work of beginning writers. I could have changed Chapter 1, *Dear Stranger* from limited omniscient to omniscient by inserting after paragraph 12,

The lieutenants had also noticed the two pretty girls, and the dark-haired one started watching Bonnie after she had turned back to Maxine.

and after paragraph 14

A gunner-sergeant who had been a jockey in civilian life left his beer behind to walk over to the girls' booth.

Each of these additions contains information that Bonnie did not have, and the story would not be in her limited viewpoint if this information were used.

A more acceptable use of omniscient is limiting the viewpoint to one person at a time, often by chapter. This is probably the point of view method most used by novelists.

Dear Stranger, taken as a whole, is omniscient because it contains sections from several different limited omniscient viewpoints. I chose to use Bonnie's viewpoint in all the scenes where she was present. However, I felt the story was expanded and enriched by eventually showing some scenes where she did not appear. They offer information to the readers which she did not have.

Omniscient viewpoint also allows the author to give information not coming from *any* of the characters. This is authorial interference, not forbidden, but to be handled carefully. Be sure to separate it from a limited viewpoint section.

Combination

Often camera and/or omniscient viewpoints are used to open a story, which then moves into a limited viewpoint, as shown in the opening paragraphs of both Part I and Part II of *Dear Stranger*. I used authorial interference in *Dear Stranger* only in the opening paragraphs of Part I and Part II.

PART I - THE FORTIES (opening sentence)
She was young in 1943—when the girls were red-lipped and virginal, and the measure of time was the duration.

PART II - THE SEVENTIES
This soldier was ten feet tall. His sleeves were rolled above his elbows, wrinkled and saturated with the sweat of honest labor. The muscles in his arm bulged from the grip on his heavy musket. The other hand lay on the handle of a resting plow. First things first.

"COMING NEXT YEAR—1776-1976 AMERICAN BICEN-
TENNIAL," the sign said.

He was the only soldier in sight as he kept his watch from
the side of a Manhattan building. On the street below his
countrymen jostled, ran over, mugged, cheated, annoyed,
chased, helped, supported, loved, and lusted after each other
in their daily quest to find themselves, do their own thing,
get a piece of the action, get it all together, find the good life,
and form a meaningful relationship.

Notice the symmetry of similar beginnings in the two parts of
the novel. In both cases the readers are given a very brief
introduction to the time setting. This is not tied in with any one
character, and is clearly information coming from the author.

A word of caution is called for here: be wary of long
introductions. Many fiction writers feel the need of explaining
what the novel is going to be about, and why it was written,
setting up the mood as it were. Write this and get it out of your
system if you must, but be prepared to have an editor discard it,
asking you to get on with the action. A story well told doesn't
need a lengthy introduction. Dramatization will do it better. If
you have read *The Woman I Am* you will notice that the
opening was changed in *Dear Stranger* so that the action
began after one sentence. All authorial comment was removed
from the opening camera eye description. The quote below is
the opening from *The Woman I Am*. I was rather fond of this
reminiscence about the forties, and hated to part with it, but I
am convinced that the new version is an improvement. I
rewrote it for *Dear Stranger* at the insistence of my Warner
editor that I start the action sooner. Compare the two to see
how authorial comment was removed, and description was
incorporated into a more active format.

Beyond the fringe of dirty snow left by a transient February
thaw, the revolving door dragged its muddy rubber stripping.

The heavy door propelled the hungry and thirsty; the lonely, the scared; the hopeful, the happy; the horny and the homesick into the warm confusion of the Wheatland Hotel's Comanche Room in midtown Lancaster.

A blur of voices rose and fell over the clink of silverware and glass, accompanying the smooth sweet swing that flowed from the jukebox where the easy loping rhythm of "Paper Doll" alternated with the sophisticated syncopated sounds of "Tuxedo Junction" and "String of Pearls." Their notes were as neatly clipped and in place as a GI haircut.

The aroma of onions and hamburger and fresh baked apple pie drifted from the booths on the restaurant side of the room. On the other side a misty veil of cigarette smoke hung over tables heavy-laden with Schlitz and Pabst Blue Ribbon. The slim red and blue draperies hanging at each break in the venetian blinds cried for attention in a sea of olive drab. Here and there a bright hair bow or feminine blouse softened the military climate.

A fluttering crepe-paper streamer on the high register validated the moving heated air that rushed to augment the warmth of human bodies mingling in the crowded room. They were apart, a more diversified group than had ever gathered in the Comanche Room at one time before Pearl Harbor. Yet they were together. They reached out to each other in shared desperation—to salvage sanity, to grasp at joy, to ferret out a little piece of normality—in a world broken loose from its axis: a world spinning in space for an isolated interval labeled "the duration." They were the youth whose horizons were bounded by the duration, when people ceased living their separate lives and gathered together to watch the receding rails of their nonstop star-spangled victory train.

February 1943 Friday
Two women emerged from the groaning revolving door and paused to look around the crowded Comanche Room. (*The Woman I Am*)

Now reread the opening page and a half of *Dear Stranger* to see how the readers are taken into the active voice sooner.

Personal Point of View

We all write about things we have experienced or heard about or fantasized. The easiest way to get inside your character is to write about someone who is very much like yourself. The point of view then *will* be the author's, but you will still be dramatizing, showing. One danger in copying yourself, or someone you know, too closely is that you may be timid about letting your imagination go; about allowing the character license to be different, to do things the real life person hasn't done, or maybe wouldn't do. Once you slacken your inhibitions this should cease to be a problem. What an opportunity to adjust fate, to say what you "shoulda said," to try out the things that "might have been." Fiction writing is creative lying, isn't it?

The next step is trusting yourself to assume a point of view that is not the same as your own. This can also be an adventure, and a test of your ability to understand how other people think and feel.

Summary: Types of point of view.

Camera: Outside eye, like movie or play. No inner thoughts. Distance. Mystery.

Omniscient: All seeing, all knowing. Everybody's thoughts. Best used in a novel with different viewpoints in different chapters (essentially serial limited omniscient) where changes from one mind to another are not too close together.

Authorial comments, coming straight from author, should be separated and justified.

Limited Omniscient: Out of one person's head; can only show what this one person knows. All description, dialogue, etc. as this one person perceives it. Creates great empathy between reader and this character.

Can be either first person (I) or third person (he, she). First person narration must be in the narrator's voice as well as through the narrator's eyes; think of vocabulary and manners of speech.

First person narrator can be either major or minor character.

Assignment:

Rewrite a familiar story—fairy tale, nursery rhyme, etc. from the following six different points of view:

1. Camera eye.

2. Omniscient.

3. Limited omniscient third person.

4. Limited omniscient first person.

5. A different character limited omniscient third person.

6. A different character limited omniscient first person.

I ask you to use a familiar, simple story so you won't need to think about anything except point of view. This is a very important exercise; I think you will understand point of view much better after you have completed it. To assist you, I am furnishing an example that I have done with the nursery rhyme, "Little Miss Muffet."

Example:

1. Camera eye:

A small girl approached a stool and eased herself down onto it. She was carefully balancing a bright blue bowl almost full of pale cottage cheese. She picked up the silver spoon that was in the bowl and, with a satisfied smile, raised the first bite to her lips. She could not see the black insect, balancing on many thin legs, that scurried along the floor behind her.

The spider moved up next to the girl and stopped dead still. When the girl at last turned her eyes in the spider's direction, she let out a shriek and leaped to her feet, sending the bowl smashing to the floor, curds and whey soiling her pretty dress. She ran from the room, disappearing down the hall.

2. Omniscient:

A little girl who looked like she was about ten years old walked into the kitchen while the cook was out of the room and helped herself to a bowlful of curds and whey. Some people call this cottage cheese. She pulled out a stool (known in the old days as a tuffet) and sat down to eat.

"This is very good curds and whey," she thought. She ate hurriedly, because she was afraid the cook would come back and catch her. She didn't know that the cook had gone to a movie and wouldn't be back until late.

A little black spider who was hungry and looking for a juicy fly, crawled off the bottom of the table and stopped on the table at the bowl's edge, wondering what the obstacle was he had come up against.

Miss Muffet saw the insect next to her plate and it about scared her to death. She jumped up and ran out of the room.

3. Limited omniscient third person:

Little Miss Muffet, who was particularly hungry today, had been watching all afternoon to see when the cook left, so she could sneak into the kitchen and find something to eat. When she at last went into the empty kitchen, she opened the refrigerator door and discovered some chilled curds and whey in a blue bowl. Just what she wanted!

She pulled out a stool, just the right height she thought, and carefully sat down on it, balancing the blue bowl on her lap. The curds were delicious, she savored every bite.

A slight movement on the floor beside her attracted attention. A glance was repeated for a closer look, and her heart leapt to her mouth when she realized the black spot on the floor was a giant spider. She had been bitten by a spider when she was very small, and nothing could frighten her more. The bowl went sailing across the floor as Miss Muffet fled to the door and down the hall, where she could be safe in her own bedroom.

4. Limited omniscient first person:

I was incredibly hungry that hot afternoon, as I saw the cook get into her old car and drive away. I figured she would be gone long enough that I could raid the ice box for a snack. She was a tough old biddy, and would never give me anything to eat between meals.

I went into the big kitchen to see what I could find. I pulled open the heavy door and on the middle shelf saw a little blue bowl filled with fresh white curds and whey.

I looked around for a place to sit down and enjoy my prize, and found a small stool in the corner that was just right. The curds and whey was delicious and I savored every bite.

When I was just a small child, I was once bitten by a spider, and I have this terrible phobia. When I looked up and saw a big black insect sitting right beside me, I completely lost control, dropped the bowl and ran out of the room.

Now I am sitting on my bed, facing this terrible internal conflict. Do I let cook find the mess on her kitchen floor and come after me, or do I go back to clean it up and face the danger of meeting the spider again?

5. A different character limited omniscient third person:

Geraldine had been the Muffet's cook for only six months, but she had firmly established her domain in the kitchen. She liked her job, and took great pride in the quality of the meals she served, but she was not at all fond of the children of the household. She never allowed them to run loose in her kitchen, or to find snacks for themselves.

One day when she had started to the grocery store, she had to come back for the list she had left behind. She heard noises in the kitchen, so walked quietly up to the door to peek in to see who was in there. She saw the blonde curls of little Miss Muffet, who was sitting on a stool eating something out of a blue bowl.

Geraldine was going to holler at her but she held back the sound when she noticed a big black spider crawling along the table. This little one was going to get just what she deserved!

Geraldine knew Miss Muffet was deathly afraid of spiders, and Geraldine was not about to rescue her.

She didn't have to wait long before Miss Muffet let out a scream, knocked the bowl from the table, anc ran out the opposite door. Even cleaning up the mess was worth it, Miss Muffet wouldn't be back soon.

6. A different character limited omniscient first person:

I think my long black legs are quite handsome. It was a terrible shock for me to learn that the world is full of giants who are afraid of me. The silly things scream and holler and run away.

For instance, just today I was strolling along, minding my own business, wishing I had a nice juicy fly to snack on. I sat down to rest beside a big blue shiny wall, and suddenly the wall went flying away and I saw a big girl screaming and running. I looked around to see what she was afraid of, but there was nothing in sight to cause such a commotion. I'm so much littler than she is, I don't see how it could be me, but maybe it was.

Lesson 6

Show, Don't Tell
The Five Senses
Active Verbs

Scenes that are dramatized, with action and dialogue, are the real meat of your story. They involve the reader more than information that is handed them by the author, already accomplished. It is not possible to dramatize every moment, however, and important decisions must be made about information that will be summarized and passed over quickly, and the more interesting moments which will be dramatized. Put yourself in the readers' shoes and ask which events you would like to witness in their entirety if you were reading this story. The details that are difficult to write may be the ones that readers would relish the most. I remember my professor telling me, "You gave half a page to a description of the phonograph, and two sentences to the love scene." He had figured out that my own inhibitions had something to do with this choice. I needed to remember that I *was* writing a love story.

See, hear, touch, taste, smell. Find the expression that will release these sensory responses in the reader. Active verbs ("Her eyes *danced*") *show* more than passive verbs followed by an adjective ("She *was happy*.") Readers have an image of her eyes dancing, but her being happy doesn't relate to any of the five senses. "The fragrence of baking apples filled the kitchen" triggers an actual smell. "The pie smelled delicious" is indefinite and inactive. What does "delicious" smell like? *Show* something *doing* something.

In the last example we learned that The Comanche Room in the Wheatland Hotel was divided into two sections—one for eating and one for drinking. It was filled with soldiers. You were not told any of these things. Sound, sight and smell show it instead.

Mixed voices rose and fell over the clink of silverware and glass—noise overlaid with smooth, sweet swing flowing from the jukebox, horn notes as neatly clipped and in place as a G.I. haircut.

The men of the U.S. Army Air Corps colored the room olive drab; the bright dots were hairbows and skirts and an occasional civilian necktie. Savory smells of hamburger and onions and fresh-baked apple pie drifted from booths. Up front a veil of smoke hovered over tables weighted with Schlitz and Pabst Blue Ribbon.

Verbs are all active, the nouns are *doing* something: rose and fell, flowed, colored, drifted, hovered.

Don't name the emotion the character is feeling, but describe an action resulting from it. Not "She was suddenly angry," but "Her jaw tightened."

Don't say she saw something (name), rather describe the thing she sees. If we are in her point of view we already know she is seeing it. After the sergeant has left, and Bonnie and Maxine have talked about men and the war, Bonnie turns her attention to the returning waitress.

As the waitress turned, a man's hand touched her drooping shoulders, a handsome gold watch showing from beneath a wool sleeve. Looking above wide shoulders, Bonnie contacted blue eyes that looked into hers and held. She recognized the dark-haired lieutenant she had been watching earlier.

The reader is there, having the experience along with Bonnie, not just listening to someone tell about what happened. The actual sequence of the movement of Bonnie's eyes is followed—waitress, hand, watch, sleeve, shoulders, eyes—and holding.

And after you have done all this showing, *don't* yield to the temptation to sum everything up for the readers, just in case they didn't get it!

Example: (a rewrite of a scene in *Dear Stranger* inserting the author's voice. Note excessive use of passive [to be] verb "was")

THIS IS *TELL:*

From their booth in the Comanche Room, Bonnie looked up to see the lieutenant she had been watching across the room.

He put his hand on the tired waitress' shoulder and said to Bonnie and Maxine, "Excuse me, before you order, how about considering the case of three lonely soldiers? It's two long hours until curfew."

His voice was cultured, he sounded like he was from the East. He was so handsome the girls were flustered, even the waitress.

He said to her, "Can you take the order at our table, if these ladies will join us?

"I'm John," he said to them, and Maxine said, "I'm Maxine."

Bonnie knew he had been watching her. She wanted to go with him, but was afraid he would think she was easy, so she said, "I'm sorry, but we really should be going." She knew Maxine was upset.

John was persistent. He said, "Please come. Just for a beer. We won't even ask your last names. A month from now you won't remember, but we will."

"We really shouldn't."

John knew she didn't mean it. He reached for her coat.

"That's not my table," the waitress said. She looked disappointed. Bonnie was sorry for her.

John took Bonnie's coat. There was a strong attraction between them, a sexual excitement. They already felt closer, a little self-conscious. Maxine pulled her coat about her shoulders and picked up her hat. Bonnie was too distracted to hear what Maxine was saying.

In the small space in front of the jukebox, a couple danced. They had just met each other, too, as coupling was often quick and temporary during World War II.

THIS IS *SHOW* (the scene as it actually appears in *Dear Stranger*):

Their waitress sidestepped a grope as she came back for their order, and Bonnie and Maxine asked for coffee.

As the waitress turned, a man's hand touched her drooping shoulders, a handsome gold watch showing from beneath a wool sleeve. Looking above wide shoulders, Bonnie contacted blue eyes that looked into hers and held. She recognized the dark-haired lieutenant she had been watching earlier.

"Excuse me." His voice was pleasant and low, a clipped accent separating the words. "Before you order, how about considering the case of three lonely soldiers. It's two long hours till curfew." He turned back to the waitress and smiled as he asked, "Can you take the order at our table—that is, if these ladies will join us?"

The waitress straightened her apron and fluttered her hand across the crooked hair net. He turned back to Maxine and then to Bonnie. "I'm John," he said.

Bonnie heard a distant voice saying, "I'm Maxine."

If we had gone straight home tonight this wouldn't be happening. He has been watching me. He saw me reject the sergeant. She said, "I'm sorry; we really should be going."

Maxine frowned and squirmed.

Placing both hands on the table edge, John leaned down. She strained to catch his words, "Please come. Just for a beer.

We won't even ask your last names. A month from now you won't remember, but we will."

I'll remember. I'll remember. "We really shouldn't, but —."

John straightened up and reached for Bonnie's coat.

"That's not my table," the waitress said. She looked tired again.

"Thank you, you've been very helpful," Bonnie said. She felt a ridiculous impulse to embrace the girl.

John folded her coat across his arm. The fur clung to the wool uniform, filling in the spaces between his arm and body. Bonnie slid from the booth into the aisle. Their eyes met and turned away.

Maxine pulled her coat about her shoulders and, chatting comfortably, picked up her hat. Bonnie heard not a word.

Crossing near the jukebox, they sidestepped a dancing couple. "What did you say you did before you got drafted?" she heard the girl ask as they glided by.

Note: The "Show" version given here could be a rewrite of the "Tell." After you have gotten the story line down you will return to improve it, applying some of the things you know about technique. Don't lose spontaneity in the first draft by trying to remember all the rules; they will eventually become an automatic part of your creating.

Assignment I:

1. Compare the preceding examples. Which one involves the reader more, is more entertaining? Why?

2. List sentences from TELL opposite sentences from SHOW that give the same information.

Example:

>   Tell: He was so handsome the girls were flustered, even
>   the waitress.
>   Show: The waitress straightened her apron and fluttered her
>   hand across the crooked hair net.

3. List conflicts and tensions occurring in this short sequence. Which are external, which internal?

4. What characteristics of Bonnie and John have you picked up without being told?

5. Is a theme emerging? (Hint: the theme is written out in TELL.)

Assignment II:

Rewrite the following limited point of view sequence with active verbs, and sensual connotations:

When Joe left work that night he felt lousy. He was the last one to leave the office which looked empty and lonely. He came out of the hot building into a cold, January night. He saw a pretty girl chasing her hat in the wind, but decided not to help her. His car was cold and almost didn't start. He had had a fight with his wife that morning, and dreaded going home. He turned off the switch in the car and went back to the all night diner (or bar—your choice) on the corner, which was warm and cozy. Inside he saw the girl who had lost her hat, sitting alone.

REMEMBER— Show, don't tell. Show something doing something. See, hear, touch, taste, smell.

Lesson 7

Dialogue

Art is more real than life. Written dialogue isn't true speech, but it must sound like it is. Written dialogue distills the dull, irrelevant talk out of conversation.

Dialogue should fit the speakers—their vocabularies, their personalities. What kind of swear words would they use? How frank are they? How do they relate to the person they are talking to? Watch out for often repeated words and expressions throughout your writing. These are your words, not theirs.

People speak in incomplete sentences. They usually contract their verbs (can't, not cannot). Long, unbroken quotes sound unnatural.

Try reading aloud the dialogues you have written. Are they comfortable? Are there too many syllables? Take some out until the rhythm seems natural.

Constantly indicating a particular speech peculiarity for a character such as a foreign accent ("geeve me your reeng"), southern dialect ("heah's mah brothuh now") or slovenly speaking ("I'm goin' home") can be very disconcerting for a reader, diverting attention from the content of the story. An occasional spelling out of these pronunciations can plant the idea in the reader's mind, without your having to spell it out every time. In *The Woman I Am*, the corporal in the opening scene dropped all the final "g's" in his speeches. When rewriting for *Dear Stranger* I decided this was too much distraction from what he was saying. The corporal became a sergeant, and was allowed to say "gonna" and "fella," but I trusted that this would be enough.

Speech tags keep the reader informed about who is speaking. Keep them simple. If we can tell who is speaking by what they are saying, tags may not be needed at all. The word "said" is unobtrusive and can be repeated over and over again. "Asked," "replied," "added" can be used occasionally. Avoid complicated tags such as "expostulated." It usually isn't a good idea to use verbs: she "laughed," "cajoled," "complained." She doesn't laugh words, and the cajoling and complaining should be shown in what she said, not needing to be explained by the author.

A bit of action by the person speaking inserted separately in the same paragraph as the quote identifies the speaker, adds a visual note, and indicates a pause. Get in the habit of using this device, it's a good one. The little actions, coming along with the dialogue, involve the readers and provide them with a moving image.

Across the table Ed stood up and reached for his coat. "If you folks can manage without me, I think I'll cruise."

Bonnie said, "We didn't mean to leave you out."

"That's all right, honey. There's bound to be something stirring around here. They can't all be nice girls."

"Don't you like nice girls?"

"They're okay when you've got the time." He stood holding the coat like a sad child. "See you guys at the bus."

Bonnie and John watched him walk with a little restless bounce through the congested room. He slowed once as he eyed a girl with curly red hair sitting in the far corner. The girl looked at him, but she was not alone, and Ed put on his coat and went out the door.

John leaned back in his chair. "Just think, an hour ago I didn't know I'd be sitting here with you."

"A development not entirely out of your control."

He grinned and cocked his head. "Well, maybe I give fate a little push now and then, but I don't give her any trouble when she pushes back."

Timing is important in dialogue passages. A pause can *show* what a character is feeling as well as words can. The author doesn't want to keep saying "she was quiet for a moment" or "there was a short silence," although occasionally these phrases will work. The insertion of action with dialogue is another way to *show* the pauses in conversation. Look back at the above example. Each little piece of action gives the impression of a break in the sound of speech. Read your dialogue aloud and check the timing. It's easy to slow it down or speed it up by realigning the action, as well as by changing the words themselves.

"Just think, an hour ago I didn't know I'd be sitting here with you."

[quick response] "A development not entirely out of your control."

[pause] He grinned and cocked his head. "Well, maybe I give fate a little push now and then, but I don't give her any trouble when she pushes back."

Interior monologue and stream of consciousness are terms used for the quoting of words from the mind of a point of view character. They can be set off in various ways as long as you are consistent throughout each story. Quotation marks are correct, but they can cause confusion between spoken and unspoken dialogue. Italics (shown on the typewriter by under-lining) are used in *Dear Stranger*.

Bonnie heard a distant voice saying, "I'm Maxine."

If we had gone straight home tonight, this wouldn't be happening. He has been watching me. He saw me reject the corporal. She said, "I'm sorry, but we really should be going."

As mentioned in the last chapter, it is not possible to "show" *everything* with dramatization and dialogue. You will need to decide what happenings are less important so that they can be summarized in exposition. In *Dear Stranger* I did this first at the beginning of Chapter 2.

Bonnie and John met for steaks and a movie on Saturday night with Joe and Maxine. On Sunday afternoon, bundled against the cold, the two of them explored downtown Lancaster, window-shopping at Murray and Penn's, walking the paths of the university campus, and arriving at the capitol building in time for a tour. They talked tirelessly, comparing and contrasting their lives and their dreams. Their fathers both had fought in World War I. His mother went to finishing school, hers hadn't finished high school. Her grandparents were farmers, his were sailors and city landlords. They both liked Tchaikovsky, Clark Gable, and rhubarb pie. Also school, October, and Richard Halliburton.

This is "telling" in its acceptable form. It is a summary of information that is used as a transition from one dramatized scene to another. "Telling" as a part of dramatization and dialogue however (as in the bad example in Chapter 8), lessens the immediacy of the action and the readers' involvement.

In the following examples, dialogue is again interspersed with action, not exposition.

Examples: They cut through the park, strolling under trees and past bushes heavy with ice. They stopped to rest at a concrete picnic area, sitting on the cold bench and leaning back against the table.

"I'll bet you forgot the watermelon," John said.

"Thought you were bringing it," she answered.

"It had to stay in the Frigidaire as long as possible. One hundred in the shade today." He placed a gloved hand over her mitten on the bench between them. "I never could stand the heat. Think of me when you share the melon with some other soldier next summer."

"Can't kid me," she whispered because he was coming closer. "There isn't any next summer."

Their first kiss barely touched, fragile, a small spark in a freezing night. "Yes there is, Bonnie. That's the way it works." He kissed her again. "Hot and cold."

She stood up, stepped onto the dead grass, the frosted blades crackling under her boots. John sat on the bench watching, then followed. He matched her slow steps. "What's the matter?"

She shook her head. They stopped and looked back at the cold, white picnic table, silent and empty.

"It looks like a statue," John said.

She shivered. "It looks like a tomb."

"It was alive when we were there."

"Were we ever there?"

"Yes, Bonnie. We were. Don't forget."

John walked over to change the record. "Clair de Lune" had been repeating for twenty minutes. He switched the machine off and stood with his back to her. The light from the street sliced through the venetian blind, casting diagonal lines across the rug.

"How long does it take to get married here?" he asked.

Sitting in the dark, Bonnie's hand went to her throat.

He spun around and she jumped. "I mean, is there a waiting period? How long?"

It wasn't the right question, but she followed his lead. "Three days."

"Tomorrow's Wednesday. I could get a weekend pass. Can't be sure, but it looks like we'll be here till next week." He took a step, then faltered. "God A'mighty, it would be a dumb thing to do!"

He walked over and switched on the lamp. He was restored to her sight, as exciting as the feel of him in the dark. Bonnie straightened and put her hands to her hair.

John's thoughtful gaze moved from her to the muted landscape print hanging above the sofa, to the crushed, petal-dotted pillows at the end, down to the worn leather footstool, over the untouched plate of cheese on the table, and back to her.

"Well, when you make up your mind, let me know." Bonnie's nervous laugh slid into a hiccup.

"Let's do it," he said. "Let's be idiots and do it."

Assignment:

Write a dialogue sequence for the story beginning you rewrote
in Lesson 6. This will be a conversation between Joe and the
girl he sees in the allnight diner or bar.

Lesson 8

Sex Scenes

Composing their first sex scene is part of the baptism of emerging fiction writers. The love scene's relative importance to the development of character, theme, and plot determines the amount of space it requires. A love story without love-making is in trouble. On the other hand insertion of a little sex, just to spice things up where it has no relevance, is offensive.

Fully rounded characters share their feelings about private matters. Whether the scene is described in a beautiful or in a crass way is a point of view problem. The scene is not a reflection of the author's personal morality; rather it is an accounting of the way this action is viewed by the point of view character. However, the author *does* have choice and control over how explicitly the scene will be dramatized.

Sex scenes in *Dear Stranger* are not totally explicit, and they are relatively "clean" because the point of view character finds them pleasing. Please note, however, the differences in tone in the different situations as the point of view character grows or changes.

Bonnie is twenty-one, she and John have just met, it is 1943:

That night, in a room lighted only by the glow of the fireplace grate, his hand sliding down her bare arm, gently touching a cheek before a kiss, resting upon a wool-skirted thigh, cradling an uncovered breast, stirred excitement she hadn't dared dream of. In past experience, touching had set off alarms, produced shields. Tonight touching opened doors through which she dared not—would not—pass.

Bonnie and John have taken out the marriage license, still
1943:

They moved to the sofa, and he unbuttoned her blouse and
pushed up her brassiere, touching and kissing her breasts for
the first time with the lights on. She was fascinated to watch
his long fingers cup the little mounds, and wondered how he
knew to brush the nipples so lightly instead of squeezing and
hurting as had happened to her before. The sight of his
moving hands excited her, made things happen lower, under
her skirt. John loosened his tie and top shirt buttons and
undid her bra in the back. She was passive at first, but
discovered that her enjoyment increased when she felt his
ear, or stroked the stubble hair above it, or slid her hand into
his shirt and found hair again—soft and curly on his chest.
They continued to kiss and stroke, and occasionally to talk,
until it was time for him to leave. They never touched, or
disturbed their clothing, below the waist.

1975: Middle-aged lovemaking. Bonnie has left her husband,
John is still married. They meet for the first time since their one
night reunion in the New York hotel.

The room was crowded with the mature, self-aware persons
they had become, the kids who shared their love on an icy
night shadowed by war, the couple who joined in adultery in
a New York hotel last spring. These persons looked at each
other with curiosity and some embarrassment, and wondered
what to say.

He said, "You've traveled with me a great deal since last
spring. I keep finding you in every revolving door."

She answered. "I've never been without you."

She extended her arms, palms up, curling beckoning
fingers selfward. He moved in beside her and they sat
together on the sofa. Their scenario developed in separate

acts with intermissions of kissing. Talk awhile, touch awhile. She kicked off her shoes and curled her feet beneath her. She helped him get rid of his coat. The vest and tie were loosened and her blouse became disarranged as they first tested the magic in their fingers through cloth.

He told her he had taken up flying again—being invaded at first by unanticipated nightmares about flak and bombs— soon moving on to a new sense of freedom, of escape for him. He was trying to cut back on his case load, he said, wanting to live before he was old, but it was difficult.

His hands were warm against personal flesh by the time she spoke of her smothering. How the anonymity of city crowds had given her solitude to find herself.

The objects in the room were disintegrating into outlines to their night-adjusting eyes when they opened up the sofa bed and took off their clothes to meet again at last, skin to skin.

The months of sleeping alone had stored up a hunger in Bonnie that exploded like skyrockets, bursting again and again, sending showers of sparks into all the extremities, leaving toes and lips alive with all the little needles, fading slowly to weakness and overpowering love for the man who had brought it all to finale.

They lay quietly for a long time afterward, on their backs close together, her head on his arm.

"I'm not the girl who gave you her virginity."

"I loved her too." He brushed his lips across her forehead.

The most explicit sex scene in *Dear Stranger* is between Bonnie's ex-husband, Frank, now in his sixties, and Bonnie's twenty-five year old neighbor, Hannah. Hannah is the point of view character in this chapter. She is a nice girl of the 1970s, no stranger to casual sex, but genuinely interested in this sophisticated, successful, older man. She has accepted his offer to meet him in Washington, D. C., although they do not yet know each other well. They return to her hotel after dinner.

They rode up silently in the elevator, and she started to put the key in the lock, saw Frank's extended hand and gave it to him instead. He unlocked the door, pushed it open and stepped back.

Inside, she flipped the switch that lit the large lamp on the dresser. Frank walked over and laid down the key. He turned without overture, reached out and pulled her toward him. He kissed her, then turned to switch off the lamp at its base. Total darkness covered them.

She felt hands, competent and sure, open up the shawl, disappear with it and come back to spread across her back and pull her very close for a longer, more open kiss.

She felt like a virgin. She hadn't been ready to lose the lights. They usually wanted to look. He tugged at the back of her blouse, pulling it up out of the wide gathered skirt and sliding his hands under it. This threw them off balance and they swayed, still glued together. Then she realized that his hands were searching for something that wasn't there. A funny little sound came from her lips. He stopped, still holding her against him.

"I don't wear one," she whispered.

He stood quite still, then said, "Oh, hell!"

The outline of the window was beginning to clear around the blind. Simultaneously they laughed. He let go and they stepped apart. Hannah crossed her arms and grasped the bottom of the blouse, pulling it over her head and tossing it toward the dresser. She could see him dimly now and she reached over and took both his hands and placed them low under her breasts, pushing up. She could hear a long, hard intake of breath. His hands slowly, gently, cupped and kneaded. His head bent down. He tasted. He was so careful she felt precious, fourteen-karat.

When he touched her skirt, she helped him push everything down together. The bunching of lined, gathered voile forced the yielding of elastic, and cobweb nylon, leaving pale, smooth flesh taut and high and round.

Frank let go of her to get out of his coat. When he raised his arms to pull off the sweater, she unfastened his belt and released his swollen sex. After dropping to the edge of the bed to get rid of his trousers, they locked together again and fell back across the bedspread. Through one long, desperate kiss, he crushed her hair and stroked her back. As he rolled to loom over her, a violence in him erupted in accelerating motion. He thrust hard, powerful, and fast. They were drenched with his sweat and he was breathing audibly when his cry turned to whimpers and the violence slowly drained out of him. She felt his weight coming down, and the gentleness returning until he was holding on instead of holding down. In time he let go and rolled over on his back, quiet. The window was a clear rectangle now, the dresser and lamp and chair all recognizable. She could see him, lying undressed beside her. He stood up and went into the bathroom.

When he came back she was still lying on top of the bed, liking what she had done for him, but disturbed and empty.

He lifted the outside of the spread and whispered, "Get under." She turned to her stomach and climbed under the covers as he turned them back, placing the pillow under her head. He slid in beside her and pulled her to him.

His two hands contacted her body, skimming the full length, up and down, arriving at the vital terminals, finding the connections, lighting the fire, starting the mounting cries of pleasure. He was taking care of her.

Much later when she was relaxed and warm, and looked after, he said, "I'm sorry I came so fast. It has been so long." He turned his head on the pillow and she knew he was looking at her in the dark. She couldn't form an answer. This was not a fuck they wrote books about. More versatile lovers she had sent packing. So what was happening to her?

She turned over and moved across. He put his arm under her shoulders and cradled her against him. They touched with their whole bodies, pushing back the lonely dark.

Each of these scenes has a different tone, reflecting the times and the stage of the relationship between the couple involved. None of the scenes is in any way extraneous to the heart of the plot. They are absolutely necessary to plot, character, and theme development.

Writing styles differ. Poetic metaphor can sometimes be used as successfully as graphic description. The last love scene in the novel between Bonnie and John is not literally described.

Their lovemaking progressed slowly, moving to the bed, inside stiff white motel sheets, sometimes slowing for words, building happily to the bursting of the rainbow, turning point, splintering hues raining over the descending action, where love became the epilogue to passion.

A sex scene from the point of view of a person who is feeling either violent or violated, who is indifferent or bored, who feels guilty or defiled, who does not respect themselves or their partner, would be told in each case in a different way. A vocabulary that names body parts, and the choice of their physiological names or various slang names, is an important tool in setting the proper tone. I suspect that my not doing any naming beyond "breast" and "nipples" is one reason The Literary Guild did not label my book "contains explicit sex."

I would hope that all my love scenes enable readers to share in intimate moments, not as intruders or voyeurs, but as participants in the experience. If I have allowed them to achieve such intense identification with my point of view character, I have succeeded as a writer. Sex is a dynamic force in life and most readers like to read about it.

Assignment:

Write a lovemaking scene for the Joe story. You will decide the circumstances under which this scene takes place. You may, if you choose, skip ahead in the story without writing the transitional material from what you wrote last. Does Joe go home and make up with his wife? Does he go home and sleep with her without making up? Does he pick up the girl for a one-night stand? Do Joe and the girl fall madly in love? You decide.

This is a good exercise, even if you never intend to write the kind of stories that call for such scenes. If it is the first time you have written one, it will be a step in overcoming your inhibitions about speaking publicly about private things, whether you are drawing from fantasy or experience (no one will ever know for sure which it is). You may be surprised at how much easier it will be to write the next one.

Note: In a classroom situation, the teacher will need to use discretion in deciding the extent to which the results of this assignment will be shared in class. Students should not be required to share what they have written if it would make them uncomfortable.

Lesson 9

Description and Symbolism

I was surprised when readers saying kind things about my book first remarked, "I particularly liked the descriptions; I knew what things looked like." I had considered myself to be an author who did not indulge in extensive description, and I had not expected them to single this out. Yet the description was there, slipped in painlessly, like the cod liver oil in the orange juice.

Long descriptive passages are easily skipped, and often are. I seldom allow myself more than one short paragraph to set up a scene.

A mantle of crystal had settled over the city. Freezing mist veiled the near and obscured the distant. Winter twilight vanquished color. Diamond trees lined platinum streets. The sidewalk stretched into a flat ribbon of ice.

Note the active verbs: "A mantle of crystal had settled over the city" instead of "the city *was* covered with ice." Every sentence presents a new specific image—crystal mantle, freezing mist, twilight, shining trees, streets, and last, the sidewalk which leads into the action immediately following. The sequence of the images is logical, as they might be taken in by the point of view character.

Often, the description can be worked in unobtrusively along with action and dialogue. It is convenient for that fill-in which will indicate transition, or the passing of time in the action or conversation.

Downtown, the few people on the street eased by like ghosts. Out of the mist the gray stone church loomed like a deserted Gothic castle. They rounded the corner, past the steep stone steps, to see a light shining through the small stained-glass windows of the chapel. Like a candle in the window at home, it drew them to the less imposing side entrance. They held each other up one last time on the stone steps, and stood tall again with firm footing in the dry hallway.

The hall was chilly, but when they passed through the heavy chapel doors, warmer air touched their stiff faces and fingers. Mellowed wood panelled the walls here, and the deep red carpet echoed the somber colors of stained-glass windows with night on the other side. Light was hushed by the amber bulbs in the antique chandelier, and the low-flamed candles in the brass candelabra.

A small man with thinning hair and glasses came toward them, his hand outstretched to grasp Bonnie's.

The action progresses throughout this description; the plot is being advanced by Bonnie and John's movement toward their wedding. When they leave the church, one sentence sets the scene again:

Sleet no longer assaulted them, but fog still lay against the buildings, absorbing the couple into its anonymous wetness.

This passage is very visual, but it is also active. The sleet and fog are characterized with active verb forms—"assaulted," "lay," "absorbing."

Symbolism

Sometimes the description has a symbolic meaning, as well as a practical one. The American Heritage Dictionary's first definition for the word "symbolism" is

1. The practice of representing things by means of symbols or of attributing symbolic meanings or significance to objects, events, or relationships.

These objects, events, or relationships have a literal purpose of their own, but, in addition, they stand for more than their literal meaning. A well written piece of fiction will often, through setting, through mood, set up symbols that weren't necessarily planned for that purpose.

I deliberately played with the descriptions of dancing in *Dear Stranger* to symbolize differences in male-female roles, as well as differences in the nation between 1943 and 1975. When Bonnie and John danced together in 1943:

The slick, quick beat of the swinging "American Patrol" intruded. Jitterbug! His hand moved from her back and quickly grasped her other hand. Without missing a step they fell into the split-second synchronization of Lindy footwork. She twisted and spun on the pivot of his wrist, flew away and back again as his strong arm reversed, the push-and-pull intercourse as intimate as a shared heartbeat. Boy, girl, and beat melted together, indivisible as the nation.

At the convention dance in 1975, Bonnie watches:

The tune was not "Speak Low." It was "Rhinestone Cowboy." A few couples moved onto the floor. They did not find each other's arms. They wiggled and squirmed and shuffled their feet. She watched a couple nearby. The young man's body writhed bonelessly, his feet barely moved. An air of lazy boredom hung about him. A few feet away, his partner wiggled and jerked, her miniskirt a half beat behind her grinding buttocks, her braless breasts vibrating to the beat of the electric guitars. *Do they know each other? They're sharing nothing.* She remembered all the times she had concentrated on missing the beat in order to follow her partner's lead. *Where he leads me I will follow. Amen.*

The changes in the styles of dancing are symbolic of the change soon to come about in Bonnie's life—asserting an independent life of her own, instead of following a man's lead all the time. The dancing also reflects societal changes brought on by the women's movement in the seventies.

When Bonnie and John are reunited that night in a hotel room, Bonnie experiences a significant change in her outlook on life (the novel's turning point). She is about to accept John's philosophy that life's choices are not black and white. "Those of us wandering in the grays have our own kinds of problems." This happened in a room described in several brief inserts scattered through the chapter:

They were in the parlor of a suite, a room of black leather, chrome and glass. . . .

The thick white carpet swallowed footsteps. . . .

She watched the circles of light from the table lamps make overlapping shadows on the thick, white carpet into varied shades of gray.

I must confess that the above example was not planned as the dancing episodes had been. I was delighted when I discovered what I had done, either accidentally or subconsciously.

At the end of that chapter (more deliberate symbolism), when Bonnie is in the cab, about to make one of the most important decisions of her life, possibly a dangerous one:

Only steps away, a New York sidewalk stretched toward an unknown horizon. The revolving door turned faster. Red lights flashed and faded on the backs of cars, on street corners, on moving neon signs.

When Bonnie is in another bleak hotel room on the night she arrives in New York alone, having left the security of husband and home behind in the midwest:

She smiled covertly and extended a timid hand to the stranger under her skin, wanting to love and guide her into a path sprouting unnamed buds.

She returned the paper and the jewelry to the box, stopping short of closing the lid. She held her left hand out in front of her and slowly spread her fingers. With right thumb and forefinger she grasped the rings and pulled. The knuckle resisted, but she pulled harder. The rings were off, leaving a white circle—exposing flesh that had long been protected. She put the solitaire and the narrow gold band into the jewelry box. Rummaging in the box, she found a ring set with two garnets. It slid backwards, too large for the ring finger. She considered whether the naked finger was too much to bear in the cold little room. Decided it was not.

The whole business of the ring suggests the throwing off of the marriage: "exposing flesh that had long been protected," and "She considered whether the naked finger was too much to bear in the cold little room. Decided it was not." These references apply to more than her finger.

One of my students pointed out some logical symbolism in the subway chapter. The pumpkin pie (no doubt homemade) that Bonnie pushed into her assaulter's face can be seen as a symbol of her dependent housewife years. She used the pie in an act of assertiveness, a symbol of her new independence. She then proceeded with confidence to settle for a New York bakery pie on Thanksgiving.

I have always suspected that many of the symbols we diligently search out for our English papers in college are not deliberately planted by the authors. My own experience bears this out. Nevertheless, however they get there, they do serve a fine purpose and enrich the non-telling impact of our stories.

Think about the symbolism of objects, settings, the weather, sub-plots (what happened to her plant or her cat). Don't get carried away with this however; the significance mustn't be strained, or too obvious. All the things described above from *Dear Stranger* are important parts of the action and none of them were inserted only to be symbols.

Sometimes a metaphor does not have a literal meaning at all ("Diamond trees lined platinum streets"). Readers know that this statement of fact is not literally true, but only symbolic.

In the example above where Bonnie removes her wedding rings, one statement is not to be taken literally:

She smiled covertly and extended a timid hand to the stranger under her skin, wanting to love and guide her into a path sprouting unnamed buds.

This one sentence suggests another meaning for the title, *Dear Stranger*, which I would have liked for people to notice. I am pleased that a number of readers have told me that they see the dear stranger as the other person in herself that Bonnie discovers.

In the scene quoted in Lesson 8, which concerns the next time Bonnie and John are together again, several months after their thirty-year reunion in the hotel room, this paragraph appears:

The room was crowded with the mature, self-aware persons they had become, the kids who shared their love on an icy night shadowed by war, the couple who joined in adultery in a New York hotel last spring. These persons looked at each other with curiosity and some embarrassment, and wondered what to say.

No reader would think that there were actually six other people in the room looking at each other with embarrassment. This fanciful metaphor is just an effective way to reconstruct Bonnie and John's shared past and to suggest their feelings at this moment. The metaphor adds variety, providing a different way than telling or showing that they were ill at ease and why.

Fanciful metaphor can be inserted effectively along with literal description and action, as long as it is growing out of the point of view character's feelings and thoughts; it is yet another way to put the reader inside the point of view character. It will not be mistaken for literal description if it is a logical statement of inner state of mind.

Assignment I:

Reassess the paragraph you wrote for the Joe story in which he first notices and enters the diner or bar. Did you, in a few well chosen words mixed with action, make the readers feel they were there? Do they know what the place looks like, what kind Can you add a fanciful metaphor that shows something about how place it is? Joe feels about it?

Example: "He slid onto a stool, workhorse turned sly tiger, drawing in his claws and purring to the pretty girl beside him, ..."

Assignment II:

Read what you have written in your own story. Can you improve the description? Will there be any symbolism? Any fanciful metaphors? Don't strain; let them emerge naturally.

Lesson 10

Some Things Not To Do

Quality fiction is noted for some things it does *not* contain. You would do well to establish warning bells in your head when you find some of the following in your rough draft.

Cliches

When a phrase emerges in your mind in one piece, examine it critically. It may be a much overworked combination, that could well be freshened by a new approach. "She walked briskly into the room, and settled herself into a chair," could be "She hurried across the room and dropped into the blue upholstered armchair with a sigh." Even "she walked into the room and sat down," would be an improvement.

Beware of "she lifted her eyes," "sank to the floor," "sprang to her feet"; or "A faint smile twisted his lips," "there came a knock on the door," "his eyes were hard as steel."

"Her voice was barely perceptible as she thought of her loved ones, fearful of incurring his wrath"—the best way to deal with this kind of language is to *simplify*. Always use the simplest words you know that will convey the meaning clearly. Change the above to, "She spoke in a small voice, remembering Joey and Meg, not wanting to make him mad." If the cliche that comes to your mind says what you want to say, just change it to simpler, less trite words that have the same meaning.

Sometimes certain types of stories are deliberately cliched. Cliches can add a comic touch or they have been used to harmonize with the mood of a formula plot, already cliched— think of some popular historical romances. This is again maneuvering technique to work for the writer. The title of this book is a cliche, designed to attract attention.

Redundancy

Showing it once is entertaining. Belaboring the point is boring.

The following example is the scene in a hotel room at II:00 PM. after Bonnie and John's hurry-up wedding the evening before his squadron ships out for England. After a few hours in the hotel—lovemaking, and some rather mundane last-minute conversation—he is leaving to go back to the base.

When she came out of the bathroom on bare feet, she stopped at the door. John stood at the window not moving, a shoe held in one hand. His shoulders were rounded, his head bent. She took a step toward him and stopped. *What is he thinking? I daren't ask.* She reached back and pulled the door shut with a click.

John straightened and looked hard out the window. He didn't say anything for a long half-minute, then smiled and said, "I do believe it's clearing. Maybe we won't be grounded after all." He sat down in the shabby chair and loosened the shoe laces.

She walked to the other chair and stroked the stiff military jacket that was draped around its back. She took it off the chair, holding it until he was ready. As she leaned her cheek against the collar, he accepted the caress with his eyes. He found the sleeves with his hands and she lifted the jacket high and wide over his shoulders. He buttoned the jacket, pulling it straight. After he picked up his cap by the visor, he laid his short coat across his arm. "Someday it will end and I'll watch you dress every day for the rest of our lives," he said.

She nodded. *Never. Never. This is the way it will always be.*

He held out his hands. She slid into her place. They tightened their hold and melted together, containing each other. He kissed her on the forehead and then on the lips. They pulled apart and he opened the door.

"Be careful," she said.

"You too."

Across the hall the elevator operator held the door. A soldier and a girl got on and turned around and watched. Three pairs of insolent, uncaring eyes blinked at them. He gave her a quick kiss, like a husband going to work, and hurried away. She shut the door before he could turn around, leaning heavily against it. *We never talked about dying.*

Slowly she moved back to the rigid armchair and lowered herself into it. Dry-eyed and wide-awake, she faced the dreary little room.

This is the end of the chapter. How easy it would be to fill up the page by adding another paragraph.

How could she face the future alone? They had only known each other for one week. Would he remember her—want to come back to her? She loved him so much. One little taste of married life, and her joy was snatched away. Of course she would be faithful. She might have to wait for years to finish the episode they had started tonight. He might not ever come back. He might die in the skies over Germany. She mustn't think of that.

The above paragraph is totally redundant. All of these things have already been established with dramatization, with action. Constant insertion of this rehashing is an easy way to make a long book; but at the risk of being redundant, I repeat—it's *boring*. Watch out when you find yourself making lists of questions that are causing conflict in the point of view character's mind. There are better ways to let the reader know about the conflict.

Repetition: Another type of redundancy that your ear will probably pick up is the repetition of a word or phrase within resounding distance of the last time it was used.

When she came out of the bathroom on bare feet, she *stopped* at the door. John *stopped* at the window, not moving, a shoe held in one hand. His shoulders were rounded, his head bent. She took a step toward him and *stopped*.

The more unusual the word, the longer it will be remembered This is the rule that allows you to use "said" without reservatior (like "the" and "in") but restricts "replied" or "exclaimed."

Watch out for the overuse of "smile," "smiled," "smiling." Your characters probably do smile a lot, but you may find this action described several times on a page, and it does get repetitive. Figure out where you can get along without mentioning it, or express the meaning of the smile in a different way some of the time.

Adverbs:

Be wary of too many adverbs. You will need a few, but they could also be redundant. They describe a verb, and often are telling instead of showing how the action is taking place. If this has already been shown, they may add nothing. The worst offenders are the "ly" adverbs. Check out the words in which "ly" has been added to an adjective which would modify a noun, to turn it into an adverb to modify a verb (excitedly, obnoxiously, happily). There are usually better ways to show that the character was excited, obnoxious, or happy. Worse yet are the "ing" plus "ly" adverbs, ("lovingly," "adoringly," "enthrallingly," "teasingly").

Especially overworked words are "suddenly," and "slowly." Find other ways to speed up or slow down the action than using these words over and over.

Remember that adverbs, even many of the above mentioned, can be used occasionally; just don't overdo it. Eliminating the excess, or making your point with the action instead of the adverb, can be another way to improve your rough draft.

Beginnings:

Don't say "she began" or "started" to do something. Just have her do it.

She walked to the other chair and *began* stroking the stiff military jacket that was draped around its back.

She walked to the other chair and stroked the stiff military jacket that was draped around its back.

Qualifiers:

Other qualifiers can be overused also. As you refine your manuscript, go hunting for overuse of "very," "really," "rather," "just," "almost," "a little bit." Usually the meaning is exactly the same without the qualifier. Read it without the qualifier and see if the meaning is changed.

Now let's see what happens when we add excess qualifiers to part of the last example.

Example:

When she came slowly out of the bathroom on bare feet, she stopped at the door. John stood at the window not moving, a shoe held sadly in one hand. His shoulders were dejectedly rounded, his head bent. She took a step toward him and stopped. *What is he thinking? I really daren't ask.* She reached back quietly and pulled the door shut with a click.

John straightened and looked determinedly out of the window. He didn't say anything for a long half-minute, then cheerfully smiled and said, "I do believe it's clearing a little. Maybe we won't be grounded after all." He sat down in the shabby chair and quickly loosened the shoe laces.

She walked to the other chair and tenderly stroked the stiff military jacket that was loosely draped around its back. She took it off the chair, holding it tentatively until he was ready. As she lovingly leaned her cheek against the collar, he accepted the caress with his eyes. He carefully found the sleeves with his hands and she sadly lifted the jacket high and wide over his shoulders. He began to button the jacket, pulling it straight. After he picked up his cap by the visor, he laid his short coat across his arm. "Someday it will end and I'll watch you dress every day for the rest of our lives," he said, tenderly.

Does this version give you any clearer picture of what is happening, or how the characters feel? Read the shorter version, repeated below, again. The scene is a poignant moment of controlled emotion, more accurately transmitted to the reader when those emotions are not named. Our glimpses into Bonnie's mind are quick flashes, without embellishment. The extra words above throw off the timing and make the scene cumbersome.

When she came out on bare feet, she stopped at the door. John stood at the window not moving, a shoe held in one hand. His shoulders were rounded, his head bent. She took a step toward him and stopped. *What is he thinking? I daren't ask.* She reached back and pulled the door shut with a click.

John straightened and looked hard out the window. He didn't say anything for a long half-minute, then smiled and said, "I do believe it's clearing. Maybe we won't be grounded after all." He sat down in the shabby chair and loosened the shoe laces.

She walked to the other chair and stroked the stiff military jacket that was draped around its back. She took it off the chair, holding it until he was ready. As she leaned her cheek against the collar, he accepted the caress with his eyes. He found the sleeves with his hands and she lifted the jacket high and wide over his shoulders. He buttoned the jacket, pulling it straight. After he picked up his cap by the visor, he laid his short coat across his arm. "Someday it will end and I'll watch you dress every day for the rest of our lives," he said.

Assignment:

Write a sketch in which you deliberately overdo all the things I have warned you not to do in this chapter. You may want to exaggerate other aspects of the story, also. At its best, this could be a funny story. At its worst, it will provide a horrible example.

Wrap-Up

Beginnings are very important. A bit of dialogue or action in the first paragraph can immediately involve readers and make it worthwhile for them to read through some necessary exposition in the next paragraph. The first sentence could be the only one readers will read if it doesn't pull them in. You will probably want to write the first sentence last, after you know what your story is. I did this with *Dear Stranger* which begins, *"She was young in 1943, when the girls were red-lipped and virginal, and the measure of time was the duration."*

Unlike expository writing, fiction does not need to be written in complete sentences. You can structure and punctuate any way you please; but as with technique, a beginning knowledge of the rules will make you much more adept at being creative with them. Keep a grammar text handy along with your dictionary. Breaking a rule must be done for a valid reason.

Basically, punctuation is there to take the place of pauses and inflections in speech. Think of a comma as the shortest pause, followed consecutively by the dash, semi-colon, colon, period, paragraph, skipped line, chapter.

Vary sentence lengths. Listen to the rhythm—the sounds the words make.

Don't be intimidated by the information in the preceding pages. I repeat, you are not writing anything in granite; you don't have to think about every rule as you write. With understanding and application, these principles will soon become automatic; but until they do, you may think more about rules as you shape and rewrite than you do while you are first drafting. Get it on paper. Don't spend too much time getting ready to go.

This is intentionally a short volume. You may want to reread it now, or after you have completed the first draft of your story. The information will become more relevant as you confront its practical application in your own writing.

Assignment I:

Finish the short story you started in Lesson 1.

First, be proud you finished something.

Next, read it as an informed critic, and think of ways you could say it better, involve the reader more. If you have some different ideas about presenting something, go ahead, give it a try.

Now, rewrite as many times as necessary to make it better. Next month you may rewrite it again. And next year again.

Assignment II:

Repeat the process with as many story ideas as you can be inspired to write.

Writing is like having a baby; it's a long hard trip, but your boundless joy in what you have created will make it a thousand times worth the pain. Only *you* could have produced these stories. You are a writer.